A RECORD OF DISCOVERY

For Exploring Computers

SECOND EDITION

Gary B. Shelly
Thomas J. Cashman
Tim J. Walker

SHELLY
CASHMAN
SERIES®

COURSE TECHNOLOGY

COURSE TECHNOLOGY
ONE MAIN STREET
CAMBRIDGE MA 02142

an International Thomson Publishing company I(T)P®

CAMBRIDGE ALBANY BONN CINCINNATI LONDON MADRID MELBOURNE

MEXICO CITY NEW YORK PARIS SAN FRANCISCO TOKYO TORONTO WASHINGTON

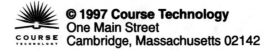

© 1997 Course Technology
One Main Street
Cambridge, Massachusetts 02142

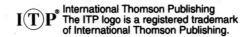

International Thomson Publishing
The ITP logo is a registered trademark
of International Thomson Publishing.

Printed in the United States of America

For more information, contact Course Technology:

Course Technology
One Main Street
Cambridge, Massachusetts 02142, USA

International Thomson Publishing Europe
Berkshire House
168-173 High Holborn
London, WC1V 7AA, United Kingdom

Thomas Nelson Australia
102 Dodds Street
South Melbourne
Victoria 3205 Australia

Nelson Canada
1120 Birchmont Road
Scarborough, Ontario
Canada M1K 5G4

International Thomson Editores
Campos Eliseos 385, Piso 7
Colonia Polanco
11560 Mexico D.F. Mexico

International Thomson Publishing GmbH
Konigswinterer Strasse 418
53227 Bonn, Germany

International Thomson Publishing Asia
Block 211, Henderson Road #08-03
Henderson Industrial Park
Singapore 0315

International Thomson Publishing Japan
Hirakawa-cho Kyowa Building, 3F
2-2-1 Hirakawa-cho, Chiyoda-ku
Tokyo 102, Japan

ISBN 0-7895-2841-X (Textbook)
ISBN 0-7895-2839-8 (Textbook and CD-ROM)
ISBN 0-7895-4355-9 (CD-ROM)

1 2 3 4 5 6 7 8 9 10   BC   10 9 8 7

Contents

Contents

Preface

A Record of Discovery for Exploring Computers, Second Edition is a journal in which students chronicle, analyze, and extend their experiences with computer concepts. The journal may be used with either the *Exploring Computers* CD-ROM or the Shelly Cashman Series Interactive Labs on floppy disk. Students investigate an interactive lab once on their own and then use this journal as they study the lab a second time. A variety of activities are provided in a format that is easy to follow and facilitates learning, helping students independently master introductory computer concepts. Each lab section in *A Record of Discovery for Exploring Computers, Second Edition* consists of four major parts:

- **Summarizing the Lab** reviews content, shows relationships, and provides additional facts in an outline that students complete as they work through the lab.
- **Evaluating the Results** tests students on their mastery of the material presented in the lab using four types of objective questions: True/False, Matching, Multiple Choice, and Fill in the Blanks.
- **Examining the Issues** challenges students to consider some interesting questions related to the lab and express their views on these intriguing problems.
- **Investigating the World** gives students the opportunity to leave the classroom and learn how people use, market, and are affected by computers.

Interspersed throughout Summarizing the Lab are features especially designed to further students' comprehension of the material presented. *Exploring Windows 95* scrutinizes each topic using the Microsoft Windows 95 operating system. *Exploring Online* suggests ways the Internet can be used to gain more information. *Exploring Your Computer* encourages students to find out more about the PC they are using.

All these elements combined provide a unique learning experience.

Acknowledgments

The Shelly Cashman Series would not be the most successful computer textbook series ever published without the contributions of outstanding publishing professionals. First, and foremost, among them is Becky Herrington, director of production. She is the heart and soul of the Shelly Cashman Series, and it is only through her leadership, dedication, and untiring efforts that superior products are produced.

Under Becky's direction, the following individuals made significant contributions to this book: Peter Schiller, production manager; Ginny Harvey, series specialist and developmental editor; Dave Bonnewitz and Greg Herrington, graphic artists; Mike Bodnar, cover design; Betty Hopkins, interior design; Patti Koosed, editorial assistant; Cherilyn King, proofreader; and Cristina Haley, indexer.

Special thanks go to Jim Quasney, our dedicated series editor; Lisa Strite, senior product manager; Lora Wade, associate product manager; Scott MacDonald, editorial assistant; and Sarah McLean, marketing director.

We hope you find using this journal an enriching and rewarding experience.

Gary B. Shelly
Thomas J. Cashman
Tim J. Walker

Shelly Cashman Series – Traditionally Bound Textbooks

The Shelly Cashman Series presents computer textbooks across the entire spectrum including both Windows- and DOS-based personal computer applications in a variety of traditionally bound textbooks, as shown in the table below. For more information, see your Course Technology representative or call 1-800-648-7450.

COMPUTERS	
Computers	Discovering Computers: A Link to the Future, World Wide Web Enhanced
	Discovering Computers: A Link to the Future, World Wide Web Enhanced Brief Edition
	Using Computers: A Gateway to Information, World Wide Web Edition
	Using Computers: A Gateway to Information, World Wide Web Brief Edition
	Exploring Computers: A Record of Discovery 2e with CD-ROM
	A Record of Discovery for Exploring Computers 2e
	Study Guide for Discovering Computers: A Link to the Future, World Wide Web Enhanced
	Study Guide for Using Computers: A Gateway to Information, World Wide Web Edition
	Brief Introduction to Computers (32-page)
WINDOWS APPLICATIONS	
Integrated Packages	Microsoft Office 97: Introductory Concepts and Techniques
	Microsoft Office 97: Advanced Concepts and Techniques
	Microsoft Office 95: Introductory Concepts and Techniques
	Microsoft Office 95: Advanced Concepts and Techniques
	Microsoft Office 4.3 running under Windows 95: Introductory Concepts and Techniques
	Microsoft Office for Windows 3.1 Introductory Concepts and Techniques Enhanced Edition
	Microsoft Office: Introductory Concepts and Techniques
	Microsoft Office: Advanced Concepts and Techniques
	Microsoft Works 4* • Microsoft Works 3.0* • Microsoft Works 2.0 — Short Course
Windows	Introduction to Microsoft Windows NT Workstation 4
	Microsoft Windows 95: Introductory Concepts and Techniques (96-page)
	Introduction to Microsoft Windows 95 (224-page)
	Microsoft Windows 95: Complete Concepts and Techniques
	Microsoft Windows 3.1 Introductory Concepts and Techniques
	Microsoft Windows 3.1 Complete Concepts and Techniques
Word Processing	Microsoft Word 97* • Microsoft Word 7* • Microsoft Word 6* • Microsoft Word 2.0
	Corel WordPerfect 7 • WordPerfect 6.1* • WordPerfect 6* • WordPerfect 5.2
Spreadsheets	Microsoft Excel 97* • Microsoft Excel 7* • Microsoft Excel 5* • Microsoft Excel 4
	Lotus 1-2-3 97* • Lotus 1-2-3 Release 5* • Lotus 1-2-3 Release 4* • Quattro Pro 6 • Quattro Pro 5
Database Management	Microsoft Access 97* • Microsoft Access 7* • Microsoft Access 2
	Paradox 5 • Paradox 4.5 • Paradox 1.0 • Visual dBASE 5/5.5
Presentation Graphics	Microsoft PowerPoint 97* • Microsoft PowerPoint 7* • Microsoft PowerPoint 4*
Personal Information Management	Microsoft Outlook 97 Mail (with Mail simulator)
DOS APPLICATIONS	
Operating Systems	DOS 6 Introductory Concepts and Techniques
	DOS 6 and Microsoft Windows 3.1 Introductory Concepts and Techniques
Integrated Package	Microsoft Works 3.0
Word Processing	WordPerfect 6.1 • WordPerfect 6.0
	WordPerfect 5.1 Step-by-Step Function Key Edition • WordPerfect 5.1 Function Key Edition
Spreadsheets	Lotus 1-2-3 Release 4 • Lotus 1-2-3 Release 2.4 • Lotus 1-2-3 Release 2.3
	Lotus 1-2-3 Release 2.2 • Lotus 1-2-3 Release 2.01
	Quattro Pro 3.0 • Quattro with 1-2-3 Menus (with Educational Software)
Database Management	dBASE 5 • dBASE IV Version 1.1 • dBASE III PLUS (with Educational Software)
	Paradox 4.5 • Paradox 3.5 (with Educational Software)
PROGRAMMING AND NETWORKING	
Programming	Microsoft Visual Basic 4 for Windows 95* (available with Student version software)
	Microsoft Visual Basic 3.0 for Windows*
	QBasic • QBasic: An Introduction to Programming • Microsoft BASIC
	Structured COBOL Programming (Micro Focus COBOL also available)
Networking	Novell NetWare for Users
	Business Data Communications: Introductory Concepts and Techniques
Internet	The Internet: Introductory Concepts and Techniques (UNIX)
	Netscape Navigator 4: An Introduction
	Netscape Navigator 3: An Introduction • Netscape Navigator 2 running under Windows 3.1
	Netscape Navigator: An Introduction (Version 1.1)
	Netscape Composer
	Microsoft Internet Explorer 3: An Introduction
SYSTEMS ANALYSIS	
Systems Analysis	Systems Analysis and Design, Second Edition

*Also available as a Double Diamond Edition, which is a shortened version of the complete book

Shelly Cashman Series – Custom Edition Program

If you do not find a Shelly Cashman Series traditionally bound textbook to fit your needs, the Shelly Cashman Series unique **Custom Edition** program allows you to choose from a number of options and create a textbook perfectly suited to your course. Features of the **Custom Edition** program are:

- Textbooks that match the content of your course

- Windows- and DOS-based materials for the latest versions of personal computer applications software

- Shelly Cashman Series quality, with the same full-color materials and Shelly Cashman Series pedagogy found in the traditionally bound books

- Affordable pricing so your students receive the **Custom Edition** at a cost similar to that of traditionally bound books

The table on the right summarizes the available materials. For more information, see your Course Technology representative or call 1-800-648-7450.

For Shelly Cashman Series information, visit Shelly Cashman Online at **www.scseries.com**

COMPUTERS	
Computers	Discovering Computers: A Link to the Future, World Wide Web Enhanced
	Discovering Computers: A Link to the Future, World Wide Web Enhanced Brief Edition
	Using Computers: A Gateway to Information, World Wide Web Edition
	Using Computers: A Gateway to Information, World Wide Web Brief Edition
	A Record of Discovery for Exploring Computers 2e (available with CD-ROM)
	Study Guide for Discovering Computers: A Link to the Future, World Wide Web Enhanced
	Study Guide for Using Computers: A Gateway to Information, World Wide Web Edition
	Introduction to Computers (32-page)

OPERATING SYSTEMS	
Windows	Microsoft Windows 95: Introductory Concepts and Techniques (96-page)
	Introduction to Microsoft Windows NT Workstation 4
	Introduction to Microsoft Windows 95 (224-page)
	Microsoft Windows 95: Complete Concepts and Techniques
	Microsoft Windows 3.1 Introductory Concepts and Techniques
	Microsoft Windows 3.1 Complete Concepts and Techniques
DOS	Introduction to DOS 6 (using DOS prompt)
	Introduction to DOS 5.0 or earlier (using DOS prompt)

WINDOWS APPLICATIONS	
Integrated Packages	Microsoft Works 4*
	Microsoft Works 3.0* • Microsoft Works 3.0 — Short Course
Microsoft Office	Using Microsoft Office 97 (16-page)
	Using Microsoft Office (16-page)
	Object Linking and Embedding (OLE) (32-page)
	Microsoft Outlook 97
	Microsoft Outlook 97 Mail (with Mail simulator)
	Microsoft Schedule+ 7
	Introduction to Integrating Office 95 Applications (80-page)
Word Processing	Microsoft Word 97* • Microsoft Word 7* • Microsoft Word 6* • Microsoft Word 2.0
	Corel WordPerfect 7 • WordPerfect 6.1* • WordPerfect 6* • WordPerfect 5.2
Spreadsheets	Microsoft Excel 97* • Microsoft Excel 7* • Microsoft Excel 5* • Microsoft Excel 4
	Lotus 1-2-3 97* • Lotus 1-2-3 Release 5* • Lotus 1-2-3 Release 4*
	Quattro Pro 6 • Quattro Pro 5
Database Management	Microsoft Access 97* • Microsoft Access 7* • Microsoft Access 2*
	Paradox 5 • Paradox 4.5 • Paradox 1.0 • Visual dBASE 5/5.5
Presentation Graphics	Microsoft PowerPoint 97* • Microsoft PowerPoint 7* • Microsoft PowerPoint 4*

DOS APPLICATIONS	
Integrated Package	Microsoft Works 3.0
Word Processing	WordPerfect 6.1 • WordPerfect 6.0
	WordPerfect 5.1 Step-by-Step Function Key Edition
	WordPerfect 5.1 Function Key Edition
	Microsoft Word 5.0
Spreadsheets	Lotus 1-2-3 Release 4 • Lotus 1-2-3 Release 2.4 • Lotus 1-2-3 Release 2.3
	Lotus 1-2-3 Release 2.2 • Lotus 1-2-3 Release 2.01
	Quattro Pro 3.0 • Quattro with 1-2-3 Menus
Database Management	dBASE 5 • dBASE IV Version 1.1 • dBASE III PLUS
	Paradox 4.5 • Paradox 3.5

PROGRAMMING AND NETWORKING	
Programming	Microsoft Visual Basic 4 for Windows 95* (available with Student version software) • Microsoft Visual Basic 3.0 for Windows*
	Microsoft BASIC • QBasic
Networking	Novell NetWare for Users
Internet	The Internet: Introductory Concepts and Techniques (UNIX)
	Netscape Navigator 4: An Introduction
	Netscape Navigator 3: An Introduction
	Netscape Navigator 2 running under Windows 3.1
	Netscape Navigator: An Introduction (Version 1.1)
	Netscape Composer
	Microsoft Internet Explorer 3: An Introduction

*Also available as a mini-module

A RECORD OF DISCOVERY

For Exploring Computers

SECOND EDITION

Using the Mouse

Summarizing the Lab

1

Instructions: Use the *Using the Mouse* interactive lab to complete the following outline.

I. What is a mouse?

A mouse is a unique _pointing device_ that fits in the palm of the hand.

Because it is used to enter data into a computer, a mouse is an example of an input device. Keyboards and scanners also are input devices.

In a _PC_, the mouse is used to select options and to move items on the screen.

A graphical user interface (GUI) makes software easier to use by incorporating icons, windows, menus, and buttons. Each _icon_ in a GUI is a small graphical symbol that represents a program or application software package, such as a word processor, or a file or document where data is stored. A _window_ is a rectangular area that presents information about an application, program, or document; a _menu_ is a list of related options. A _button_ is a rectangular, circular, or other type of icon that causes an action to take place when clicked.

Exploring Online

Early Internet software could be controlled only by using the keyboard. With modern Internet software, including Web browsers such as Microsoft Internet Explorer and Netscape Navigator, people can access text, graphics, and other types of media by pointing and clicking the mouse.

The Yahoo! home page includes a listing of home pages devoted to mouse devices and mouse accessories such as mouse pads and mouse boards. Companies such as Logitech also include pictures of different types of mouse devices on their Web sites. To learn more about using a mouse, visit the Exploring Computers Web page (www.scsite.com/expl.htm) and click Mouse.

II. Mouse operations

The primary advantage of a mouse is that it is easy to use.

A. Moving the mouse across a desktop controls the movement of a ___pointer___ (arrow) on the screen. Pointing means moving the mouse across a flat surface until the mouse pointer rests on or points to a specific object on the screen.

An electromechanical mouse has a small ball in its base. When the ball moves, a signal is sent to the computer and the mouse pointer moves accordingly. An optical mouse contains a minicamera. As the mouse moves across the surface of a special grid, the position of the mouse is conveyed to the computer.

Trackballs and joysticks also can control the movement of the mouse pointer.

Exploring Your Computer

Examine the mouse you are using to work through these labs. Do you have an optical mouse or electromechanical mouse? Does it have one, two, or three buttons? Does it have a wheel button? Are you using a mouse pad to protect your mouse from dirt and dust?

B. Moving the mouse pointer to an object on the screen and then pressing and releasing one of the buttons on the mouse is called ___clicking___ the object.

A mouse, such as the Microsoft IntelliMouse™, also can have a combination ___wheel / wheel lever___, which can be rotated like a wheel or clicked like a standard mouse button.

A typical mouse has a ___left button___ and a ___right button___, each serving a different function.

Usually, objects are clicked with the left mouse button. In some applications, pointing to an object and clicking the right mouse button reveals a shortcut menu of options related to that object This is called ___right clicking___.

___Double clicking___, which frequently is used to open a file or begin running an application, is accomplished by pointing to an object and quickly pressing and releasing the left mouse button twice.

Software applications such as Windows allow users to adjust the double-click speed of the mouse.

> **Exploring Windows 95**
>
> In Windows 95, users can right-click files, programs, and other objects to display shortcut menus (menus that apply to a specific screen or situation). These menus may include commands for cutting, copying, pasting, opening, or performing a variety of other functions on each object.

C. In a graphical user interface, _dragging_ often is used to move objects on the screen. To drag an object, point to it, hold down the left mouse button, and move the mouse pointer, to the desired location. When the mouse button is released, the object is dropped. You can use dragging to make a copy of a file on a floppy disk.

One disadvantage of using a mouse is that it requires empty desk space where it can be moved about. Another disadvantage is that the user must remove a hand from the keyboard and place it on the mouse whenever the mouse pointer is to be moved or a command is to be selected.

III. Manipulating user interface controls

A. A basic tool in a GUI is a _button_, which can be used to open a menu or a window. Clicking the Start button, for example, displays the _start menu_, which is the most basic menu in Windows 95. Most applications installed on your computer can be started from this menu.

B. A _dialog box_ may contain any or all of the user interface controls. It is a type of window with buttons or options used to modify a group of settings or enter information. In the Windows environment, a dialog box displays whenever additional information is needed.

A dialog box may contain any or all of the controls illustrated in Figure 1 on the next page.

C. An _option box_ allows you to select only one of several options.

An option button is clicked to select it. A selected option button contains a black dot. A dimmed option button represents an option that cannot be selected.

D. Other controls in a dialog box include:

- _Slider_, which you drag back and forth to change values within a range;

- _Tabs_, which allow you to move through groups of options in a dialog box; and

- _buttons_, such as OK, Cancel, and Apply, which execute an action.

E. _Drop down list boxes_ look like white boxes with text and a down arrow button. They offer a collection of items from which to select. To select an item, first click the _down arrow_ to the right of the drop-down list box to display the list, then point to the desired item and _click_ .

When the drop-down list box is clicked, the current selection is highlighted in the drop-down list. As soon as a new item is selected, the list disappears and the selected item appears in the drop-down list box. Clicking the down arrow in a list box _display_ the list so you can view different options.

F. _Option box_ act like switches. They are turned on and off by _clicking_ and can be used to select more than one option. A check mark in a check box usually indicates the option is turned on.

Dialog boxes also may contain text boxes, where text is displayed or entered, and spin boxes, which are used to scroll though values in set increments.

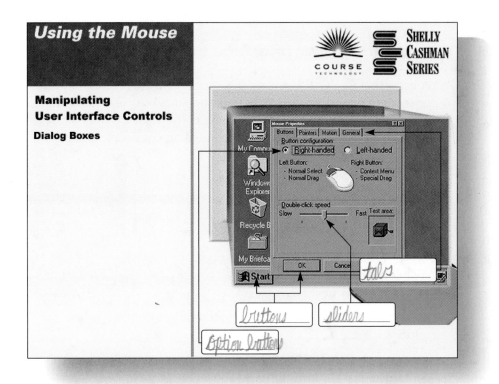

Using the Mouse

COURSE
TECHNOLOGY

SHELLY
CASHMAN
SERIES

**Manipulating
User Interface Controls**

Dialog Boxes

Figure 1

Evaluating the Results

True/False

Instructions: Circle **T** if the statement is true or **F** if the statement is false.

T (**F**) 1. When the mouse pointer is pointing to an object on the screen and then one of the mouse buttons is pressed, it is called *dragging* the object.

T (**F**) 2. To double-click an object, point to it with the mouse pointer and then press both mouse buttons at the same time.

(**T**) **F** 3. When dragging an object, the object is dropped as soon as the mouse button is released.

(**T**) **F** 4. A check box is turned on or off by clicking it.

(**T**) **F** 5. Clicking the down arrow in a list box scrolls through the options in that list.

Matching

Instructions: Write the letter of a description from the column on the right in front of each term in the column on the left.

_d_ 1. Check boxes   a. may contain several user interface controls

_e_ 2. Option buttons   b. look like white boxes with some text next to a down arrow

_b_ 3. Drop-down list boxes   c. are rectangular areas in which text is typed

_g_ 4. Sliders   d. act like switches to turn alternatives on or off

_a_ 5. Dialog boxes   e. form a group of choices from which only one can be selected

                                     f. immediately execute an action or command

                                     g. can be dragged to set a value within a range

Multiple Choice

Instructions: Circle the correct response.

1. What is mouse used for in a graphical user interface?
   a. to enter text into the computer
   b. to select options and move items on the screen
   c. to convert information on paper into digital information a computer can use
   d. to store a large number of programs and data

2. In what direction does the mouse pointer on the screen move if the mouse is moved forward (in the direction of the cable by which it is attached to the computer)?
   a. up
   b. down
   c. left
   d. right

3. What should you do if you run out of desk space while moving the mouse?
   a. slide the mouse back to its starting point and try moving it again
   b. double-click the mouse button then slide the mouse in the opposite direction
   c. move the mouse more slowly across the desk top
   d. lift the mouse off the desk top and reposition it in the center of the area

4. What mouse operation is used frequently to open a file or begin running an application?
   a. pointing
   b. clicking
   c. double-clicking
   d. dragging

5. Which of the following are used to select one option out of several in a group?
   a. option buttons
   b. check boxes
   c. sliders
   d. scroll bars

Fill in the Blanks

Instructions: Place the correct word(s) in the blank in each sentence.

1. A(n) _mouse_ is a unique pointing device that fits in the palm of your hand.

2. Moving the mouse across a mousepad or the top of a desk controls the movement of a(n) _pointer_ (arrow) on the screen.

3. To select objects such as menu commands and buttons, you _clicking_ them.

4. In a graphical user interface, _dragging_ often is used to move objects.

5. _Right clicking_ an object displays a shortcut menu related to that object.

➤1-9

Examining the Issues

1. Although the mouse was first invented in the early 1970s, its popularity grew slowly until the introduction of the Apple Macintosh computer in 1984. The Macintosh had a graphical user interface and was sold with a mouse. Today, the mouse is an almost essential input device for all personal computers; many software packages require the use of a mouse. Will the mouse still be popular thirty years from now, or will it be replaced by a different type of pointing device? Why? What factors could make another pointing device, such as a joystick or trackball, more popular than the mouse?

2. Before the advent of the graphical user interface, people had to type commands to instruct the computer to perform various tasks. For example, to delete a file named Charlie, a user would type the command, del Charlie. This method of communicating with the computer is called a command-driven interface. With a graphical user interface, however, an operator may use the mouse to drag an icon representing Charlie over an icon picturing a trash can to perform the same task. What are the advantages of using a GUI? What are the disadvantages?

Investigating the World

1. Originally, the computer mouse had a simple rectangular shape, something like a deck of cards. Today, a mouse can come in a variety of shapes and sizes and even have different numbers and types of buttons, including wheels. Using catalogs, brochures, or trade magazines, obtain pictures of at least five different mouse types. What are the advantages of each? What are the disadvantages? If you were going to purchase one for your personal computer, which would you buy? Why?

2. Instead of a mouse, some computers use other pointing devices such as trackballs or joysticks. Visit a computer vendor and find a computer that uses a pointing device other than the mouse. What kind of computer is it? What type of pointing device does it use? Why? Try using this device to maneuver the mouse pointer. Would you buy a computer with this type of pointing device? Why or why not?

Using the Keyboard

Summarizing the Lab

2

Instructions: Use the *Using the Keyboard* interactive lab to complete the following outline.

I. What is a keyboard?

A keyboard is an input device that allows users to *communicate* with a computer.

The keyboard is the most commonly used input device. Unlike the mouse, however, training is required to use the keyboard efficiently. Although all computer keyboards may seem alike, the keys on the keyboard, the placement of keys, the spaces between the keys, the feel of the keys, and the noise produced when a key is pressed may vary. As a result, operators sometimes feel that one keyboard is easier to use than another.

The keyboard is used to enter *data*, *commands*, and *responses to prompts*.

Recently, some keyboards have been designed ergonomically in an effort to minimize repetitive strain injuries such as carpal tunnel syndrome (CTS). These keyboards may use wrist rests and alternative key layouts that the manufacturers claim keep an operator's hands in more natural positions.

II. Elements of the keyboard

Five categories of keys on the keyboard are shown in Figure 2 on the next page.

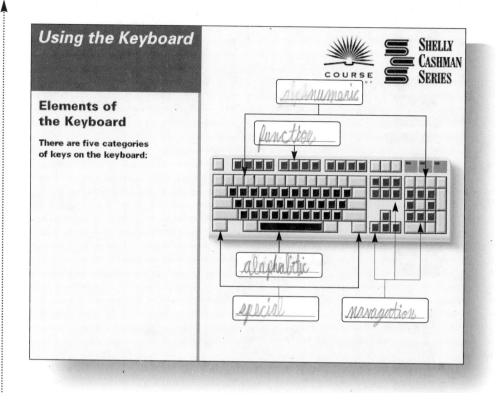

Using the Keyboard

COURSE

SHELLY
CASHMAN
SERIES

**Elements of
the Keyboard**

There are five categories
of keys on the keyboard:

alphanumeric

function

alphabetic

special

navigation

Figure 2

The position of the function keys, navigation keys, and numeric keypad
may vary depending on the keyboard's age and manufacturer. The
original 83-key IBM keyboard placed the function keys in two columns
on the left side of the keyboard. The keyboard shown in this lab is
representative of the 101-key enhanced IBM compatible keyboard.

At the top right corner of the keyboard there are also *lights (status)* .

When the computer is turned on (booted) it checks the keyboard. On
many computers, the status lights flash while this check is taking place.

Exploring Your Computer

Is your computer keyboard a 101-key IBM compatible keyboard? Is it a
larger keyboard or a smaller, portable-style keyboard? Are there status
lights for NUM LOCK, CAPS LOCK, and SCROLL LOCK? Right now, are any of
these lights on? Does your keyboard have a numeric keypad? How is your
keyboard different from the one shown in this lab?

A. The ___alphabetic keys___ are similar to those on a standard typewriter.

A modification of the conventional keyboard is available with Braille key-caps for the visually impaired. Keyboards with alternative alphabetic key layouts also are available.

There are three types of alphabetic keys: ___letter___ , ___punctuation___ , and ___space bar___ .

Some keys may represent more than one function. Alphabetic keys enter lowercase letters when the key alone is pressed, or uppercase letters if the ___shift___ key is held down while the key is pressed or if the ___caps lock___ key is pressed.

The ___caps lock status light___ indicates that the alphabetic keys will transmit uppercase letters rather than lowercase letters.

The **CAPS LOCK** key is called a toggle key because it turns on a mode when pressed and turns off the mode when pressed again. The **NUM LOCK** key and, in some software applications, the **INSERT** (**INS**) key, are also toggle keys. Unlike the **SHIFT** key, the **CAPS LOCK** key cannot be used to print the top character shown on keys with two characters (like the key with 1 and !).

B. The ___numeric key pad___ contains keys similar to those on an adding machine or calculator.

To use these keys, it is necessary to press the ___num lock___ key in the top left corner of the keypad.

When the ___num status___ is lit, the keys in the numeric keypad perform like those on a calculator.

The numeric keypad is designed for rapid entry of numeric data. Due to space limitations, portable computers (notebooks, subnotebooks, and laptops) usually do not have numeric keypads.

C. ___Navigation keys___ include arrow keys and four special keys that can be used to move through text on the screen.

An insertion point, or cursor, is a symbol that indicates where on the screen the next character typed will appear.

When the ___num lock___ key is turned off, some of the keys on the numeric keypad can be used to move the insertion point. There are dedicated arrow keys as well.

When an arrow key is pressed, the cursor moves one space in the same direction as the arrow on the key. Holding down an arrow key moves the insertion point rapidly in the indicated direction.

Four other keys can be used to navigate on the screen: ___home___ , ___end___ , ___page up___ , and ___page down___ . The functions of these keys change depending on the software application.

D. The _function keys_ along the top of the keyboard are used to accomplish certain tasks quickly.

Function keys are used mostly to transmit _commands_ to the computer.

Some software applications provide keyboard templates, which are plastic sheets designed to fit on the keyboard next to the function keys. They indicate the command each key performs.

Function keys can be _programmed_ for specific tasks.

Because of this capability, function keys also are called programmable keys, or soft keys, because their functions usually are assigned by the software package.

Some function keys have fixed meanings; other function keys mean different things depending on the software application being used. Software manufacturers have tried to standardize the purpose of a few function keys. For example, function key **F1** often can be used to obtain Help on an application.

Knowledge of the uses of function keys can save a computer operator a great deal of time. Windows applications, however, generally depend more on using icons and a pointing device than on function keys.

Exploring Windows 95

The Microsoft Natural keyboard includes three new keys that are not part of traditional computer keyboards. These keys and special key combinations trigger actions that are specifically for Microsoft's Windows 95 operating system. Some of these actions include accessing the Start menu, activating taskbar buttons, displaying the Run dialog box, and minimizing documents.

E. Depending on the application being used, the _special keys_ perform specific tasks more efficiently.

How special keys are used:

1. The _escape_ key generally is used to exit from a dialog box or an application.

2. The _ctrl_ and _alt_ keys may turn the alphabetic keys into function keys or may change their meanings in other ways.

   Usually, the **CTRL** key makes a key perform a _control_ function.

Usually, the **ALT** key gives the key an ___*alternate*___ meaning.

The **CTRL** and **ALT** keys are used like the ___*shift*___ key — by holding down the **CTRL** or **ALT** key while pressing another key on the keyboard.

Special keys that usually are used alone include **ENTER** (enters data or completes a paragraph), **BACKSPACE** (erases the character just typed), **TAB** (advances the insertion point to a defined spot), **DELETE** (erases the character to the right of the insertion point), **INSERT** (allows a character to be inserted or toggles insert typing mode on and off), and **PRINT SCREEN** (prints the current screen display or stores it in the computer's memory).

Special key combinations in the Windows environment perform specific tasks:

- ___*Alt and tab together*___ displays the list of applications that are open.
- Pressing ___*tab*___ while holding down the **ALT** key displays the name of the next open application one by one.

In the Windows environment, special keys may be used in combination with the mouse. For example, holding down the **CTRL** key while clicking the mouse button sometimes can be used to select more than one item.

Exploring Online

Many keyboard-related sites exist on the Internet. For example, the Computer Museum in Boston has a home page that shows how a giant keyboard was built as part of its Walk-Through Computer exhibit.

The Keyboard Alternatives Web site provides keyboard descriptions, graphics, and advice that can help in choosing the best keyboard for various needs. For more information on using a keyboard, visit the Exploring Computers Web page (www.scsite.com/expl.htm) and click Keyboards.

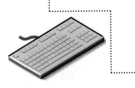

Evaluating the Results

True/False

Instructions: Circle **T** if the statement is true or **F** if the statement is false.

T (**F**) 1. Each of the many keys on a keyboard can represent only one function.

T (**F**) 2. When the **NUM LOCK** light is lit, some of the keys on the numeric keypad can be used to control the insertion point

T (**F**) 3. In general, the **HOME** key moves the insertion point to the beginning of a document.

(**T**) **F** 4. Exactly what tasks the special keys on the keyboard perform depends largely on the software being used.

(**T**) **F** 5. Usually, the **CTRL** key makes a key perform a control function, such as a command.

Matching

Instructions: Write the letter of a description from the column on the right in front of each term in the column on the left.

___ 1. Alphabetic keys
a. perform specific tasks more efficiently

___ 2. Numeric keys
b. are similar to those on a standard typewriter

___ 3. Navigation keys
c. include arrow keys and four special keys

___ 4. Function keys
d. are used to turn the computer on and off

___ 5. Special keys
e. are similar to those on an adding machine or calculator

f. are used mostly to transmit commands to the computer

g. show the status of each toggle key

Multiple Choice

Instructions: Circle the correct response.

1. Where are the status lights located on the keyboard?
   a. upper right corner
   b. lower right corner
   c. upper left corner
   d. lower left corner

2. Which of the following is *not* a type of alphabetic key?
   a. a letter key
   b. a punctuation key
   c. the **SPACE BAR**
   d. a navigation key

3. What type of keys can be programmed for specific tasks?
   a. alphabetic keys
   b. numeric keys
   c. function keys
   d. special keys

4. How are the **SHIFT**, **CTRL**, and **ALT** keys used with other keys?
   a. press a key and release it, then press the **SHIFT**, **CTRL**, or **ALT** key
   b. press a key and hold it down, then press the **SHIFT**, **CTRL**, or **ALT** key
   c. hold down the **SHIFT**, **CTRL**, or **ALT** key while pressing another key
   d. quickly press the **SHIFT**, **CTRL**, or **ALT** key simultaneously with another key

5. In the Windows environment, pressing what key combination displays the list of open programs?
   a. **CTRL+ESC**
   b. **ALT+TAB**
   c. **CTRL+TAB**
   d. **ALT+ESC**

Fill in the Blanks

Instructions: Place the correct word(s) in the blank in each sentence.

1. The _caps lock_ light indicates that the alphabetic keys will now transmit uppercase letters instead of lowercase letters.

2. To use the numeric keypad, it is necessary first to press the _num lock_ key on the numeric keypad.

3. In general, the _page up_ key moves up one screen.

4. The _function_ keys along the top of the keyboard are used to accomplish certain tasks quickly.

5. The _esc_ key generally is used to exit from a dialog box or an application.

Examining the **Issues**

1. The traditional arrangement of letters on the keyboard is called the QWERTY layout, a name that comes from the first six keys on the top row of letters. This layout, designed by Christopher Sholes in the 1800s, was developed to slow down typists and prevent the keys from jamming. Although having keys jam is no longer a problem, most keyboards today continue to use the same arrangement of letters. Yet, alternative designs are available. The Dvorak keyboard places the most commonly typed letters in the home row, or the row on which the fingers rest. The Maltron keyboard is split and shaped to fit each hand, with the most commonly used keys under the strongest fingers. What are the advantages of the Dvorak and Maltron layouts? What are the disadvantages? On which keyboard would a trained typist be able to enter the fastest input? Why? Will the Dvorak or Maltron layouts ever be widely accepted? Why or why not?

2. You can enter numbers into a computer by using either the numeric keypad or the row of numbers above the alphabetic keys. Under what circumstances would you be more likely to use the numeric keypad to enter numbers? Why? When would you be more likely to use the row of numbers above the alphabetic keys? Why?

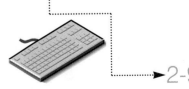

Investigating the World

1. By the year 2000, experts predict that sales of portable computers (laptop, notebook, and subnotebook) will constitute 35 percent of total computer sales. Portable computers already have the same capabilities as many desktop personal computers. Many components have been miniaturized for use in portable computers, but because the keys must be large enough to accommodate human fingers it is difficult to downsize the keyboard. A common approach taken by manufacturers has been to use fewer keys and carry out certain tasks by pressing two or more keys simultaneously. Visit a computer vendor and try two portable computers. What keys described in this lab have been eliminated on each portable computer keyboard? How are the tasks performed by these keys accomplished on each portable computer? Which portable computer is easier to use? Why?

2. Computer keyboards for some non-European based languages can be considerably more complex than the keyboards with which we are familiar. Different alphabets pose special problems for keyboard designers. For example, most Japanese writing is a combination of kanji (1,850 basic characters) and kana (additional symbols representing specific syllables), far more symbols than on our standard keyboards! Visit a library or other research facility to learn about computer keyboards used with a non-European based language. What problems for keyboard designers, if any, are suggested by the language's alphabet? How have the problems been addressed? What symbols are used on the keyboard? How are the non-alphabetic keys (navigation keys, function keys, numeric keys, and special keys) different from those on our standard keyboard?

Word Processing

Summarizing the Lab

3

Instructions: Use the *Word Processing* interactive lab to complete the following outline.

I. Word processing software

Word processing is the ability to produce or modify text to create a document.

Word processing software enables the computer to generate both a _paper_ and an _electronic copy_ of a document.

II. Word processing documents

Word processing software is used to produce:

- _Letter_ ✓
- _Newsletters_
- _memos_
- _reports_
- _web pages_
- _other doc._

III. Capabilities of word processing software

Documents are stored _electronically_, so they can be retrieved and edited quickly.

Words, sentences, or entire sections can be added, deleted, or rearranged without having to retype the entire document.

IV. Producing a document

Producing a document involves the steps described in Figure 3 on the next page.

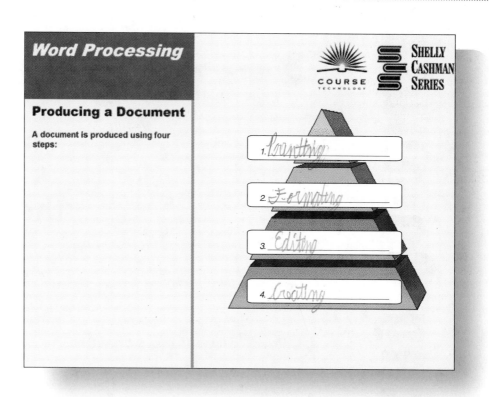

Figure 3

A. Creating a document

1. ___Wordwrap___ enters an automatic line return when the text reaches a certain position in the document.

2. A document can be viewed as one continuous piece of paper or broken up into pages.

    ___Scrolling___ is the process of moving through a document to view its various parts.

    Clicking the scroll arrows on the scroll bars shifts the document up and down or right and left.

3. The insertion point indicates where the next character will appear on the screen.

    The insertion point can be moved with a pointing device by ___clicking___ where text should be added. The ___arrow keys___ on the keyboard move the insertion point one character or line at a time. When the arrow keys are held down, the movement is repeated until the key is released.

    The ___Page Up & Page Down___ keys move the insertion point a full screen.

    The ___Home & End___ keys move the insertion point to the beginning or end of a line.

Exploring Windows 95

Windows 95 includes two applications that allow users to create simple word processing documents: Notepad and WordPad. Notepad has a very basic window with an area for text entry, a title bar, and a menu bar. All documents created in Notepad are saved as text files. Unlike Notepad, the WordPad window includes a title bar, a menu bar, *and* toolbars with buttons such as Save, Print, Copy, and Paste. WordPad also allows you to format the text and save the document in several different file formats (including Word for Windows). To start either application, click the Start button, point to Programs on the Start menu, and point to Accessories on the submenu. Click Notepad or WordPad, depending on the application you wish to start.

B. Editing a document

1. _Inserting_ involves adding text to a document. _Deleting_ involves removing text.

   Insert mode automatically moves existing text to the right as new text is typed. Typeover mode replaces existing text as new text is typed. Most word processors normally are in insert mode.

   The _Delete & Backspace_ keys provide a simple way to remove text.

   The **DELETE** key removes characters to the right of the insertion point, and the **BACKSPACE** key removes characters to the left.

2. Cutting removes selected text from a document and stores it electronically on a location called the _Clipboard_ .

   copying duplicates selected text on the Clipboard so it can be pasted somewhere else.

   In addition to toolbar buttons, most word processing programs also have an _edit_ menu that can be used to cut or copy selected text and then paste it in another location.

3. Drag-and-drop editing involves moving a part of a document by dragging it from one position and dropping it in another.

4. The _search_ feature finds all occurrences of a character, word, or group of words. The _Replace_ feature is used to replace characters or words with a new character, word, or group of words.

Some word processors also can find specific formats, use wildcards, and even locate words that sound like other words.

5. A <u>Spellchecker</u> reviews words, sections, or entire documents for correct spelling.

The <u>Automatic</u> feature fixes common misspellings, adds capital letters to the names of days, corrects two initial capital letters, and more.

A <u>Thesaurus</u> is used to look up synonyms for words in a document.

<u>A Grammer Checker</u> review grammar and check writing style and sentence structure. Most grammar checkers let users apply different rules for different types of writing (such as casual, formal, or technical).

6. New word processing programs are being geared for <u>online</u> editing.

Online editing circulates an electronic version of a document over a network, allowing people to suggest corrections or changes before a final copy of the document is printed. Often, a different color is used for each reviewer.

<u>Revision Marks</u> are used to flag additions and deletions. <u>anotations</u> are used to add comments and edits to a document. <u>Highlighting</u> is used to emphasize essential parts of a document.

7. <u>Undo</u> is used to cancel an action from a list of recent actions performed in a document.

Exploring Your Computer

Do you have word processing software installed on your computer? If so, what is the name of the application? What templates are included with the software? Does it have features such as spell check, grammar checker, and a thesaurus? Does it support online editing? What types of graphics can you insert into a document? Does the word processor automatically save documents as you work on them?

C. Formatting a document

1. <u>Type Face</u> is a specific set of characters that are designed the same.

Typefaces often are called <u>style</u>. Font sizes are measured in <u>vertical points</u>.

A font is a specific combination of typeface and point size, such as 10-point Arial.

Common point sizes used in business correspondence are _10 & 12_ points.

A point is approximately $1/72$ of an inch high. 12 points is equivalent to $12/72$, or $1/6$, of an inch.

Style is a feature that can be added to a font, such as **bold**, *italics*, or underlining.

2. Margins define the amount of empty space at the left, right, bottom and top of a document.

   Alignment is how text is positioned in relation to the right and left margins. The four common types of alignment are _left_, _Right_, _center_, and _Justify_.

3. _Spacing_ is how far apart individual letters and lines of text are placed.

   Monospacing uses the same amount of space for each character. Proportional spacing gives more space to wide characters (such as W) than to narrow characters (such as I).

   Line Spacing determines the distance from the bottom of one line to the bottom of the next line. The most common line spacings are _single & double_ line spacing.

   Some word processing software also allows exact distances to be specified, usually in points.

4. _Col._ arrange text as in a newspaper or magazine.
   Table organize text in rows and columns.

5. Most word processing programs are capable of including different types of graphics.

   Clip art usually comes in collections that are grouped by theme or description.

   Pictures also can be taken with a _digital camera_ or converted into electronic form using a scanner.

   Once a graphic is inserted into a document, it can be moved, resized, rotated, or cropped.

6. _Borders_ accentuate text, graphics, or tables with a decorative line or box.

   Shading darkens the background of an area to provide contrast.

   Colors can be applied to graphics, borders, and shading. Unless a color printer is used, however, colors will print as shades of gray.

7. _Page numbering_ is a useful feature with documents that have multiple pages.

Text also can be placed at the top of each page as a _Header_ or at the bottom of each page as a _Footer_ .

8. Formatting can be saved as a style and used in future documents.

Many word processing programs have _templates_ that use predefined styles.

Templates also include text that is always used, such as a title and headings.

Many word processing programs have an AutoFormat feature that formats documents as they are typed. AutoFormat automatically creates symbols (such as ☺ when :) is typed), fractions (such as ½ when 1/2 is typed), and ordinal numbers (such as 1st when 1st is typed).

Exploring Online

Understanding word processing means learning many unique terms, such as fonts, styles, headers, and points. PC Webopaedia — an online encyclopedia that maintains a comprehensive word processing glossary — can help you become familiar with these new terms. Once you have learned the basics, the WordInfo Web site will help you create attractive, well-written documents. To learn more about word processing resources on the Web, visit the Exploring Computers Web page (www.scsite.com/expl.htm) and click Word Processing.

D. Saving a document

Three common ways to save a document are to: _toolbar button from_ , _file menu_ , or _key combinations_ .

E. Printing a document

1. _Print preview_ shows how a document will look when printed.

2. _Portrait_ orientation prints so the document is taller rather than wider.

Landscape orientation prints so the document is wider rather than taller.

To print a document, click File on the menu bar and then click Print to display the Print dialog box.

Evaluating the **Results**

True/False

Instructions: Circle **T** if the statement is true or **F** if the statement is false.

T (**F**) 1. Word processing software is the least used productivity software, because the typewriter is used for virtually all personal and business communications.

(**T**) **F** 2. Word processing software allows words, sentences, or entire sections to be added, deleted, or rearranged without having to retype an entire document.

T (**F**) 3. As text is typed, the **ENTER** key must be pressed at the end of each line so that the text will continue on the next line.

(**T**) **F** 4. Copying duplicates a selected section of text on the Clipboard.

T (**F**) 5. Margins usually are measured in points.

Matching

Instructions: Write the letter of a description from the column on the right in front of each term in the column on the left.

_e_ 1. Creating

_b_ 2. Editing

_f_ 3. Formatting

_a_ 4. Printing

_c_ 5. Saving

a. generating one or more paper copies of a document

b. making changes to a document

c. storing a copy of a document to prevent work from being lost

d. authorizing the production of a document

e. making a document by entering text with the keyboard

f. changing the appearance of a document

g. distributing a document among coworkers and soliciting opinions

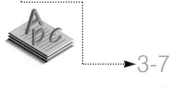

Multiple Choice

Instructions: Circle the correct response.

1. Which of the following is *not* a type of document produced with word processing software?
   a. reports
   b. newsletters
   c. spreadsheets
   d. Web pages

2. Which key moves the insertion point to the beginning of a line?
   a. **HOME**
   b. **LEFT ARROW**
   c. **END**
   d. **RIGHT ARROW**

3. What editing feature is used to search for synonyms for words in a document?
   a. spell checker
   b. thesaurus
   c. grammar checker
   d. search and replace

4. Font size is measured in what unit?
   a. points
   b. inches
   c. centimeters
   d. rods

5. Landscape orientation is used to print what type of documents?
   a. personal letters
   b. long reports
   c. interoffice memos
   d. tables with many columns

Fill in the Blanks

Instructions: Place the correct word(s) in the blank in each sentence.

1. _Scrolling_ is the process of moving through a document to view its various parts.

2. The _insert mode_ of a word processor automatically moves existing text to the right as new text is typed.

3. Most word processors have a(n) _edit_ menu that can be used to cut or copy selected text and then paste it in another location.

4. When the alignment of text is _justified_, words are spread out in each line so that the right and left margins are even across the document.

5. The _print preview_ feature shows how a document will look when it is printed.

Examining the Issues

1. Although many homes and almost all businesses in America use word processing software, people in Europe have been slower to embrace the most popular productivity software. In France, applications for schools and jobs usually are still written by hand and often with a fountain pen. Handwriting is thought to show greater formality and more personality, while documents produced with word processors are seen as impersonal. Handwriting analysis even plays a role in hiring decisions. Will word processing ever become as widely accepted in Europe as it is in America? Are documents produced with word processors more impersonal than those written by hand? Why? For what kind of documents, if any, do you feel word processors are inappropriate?

2. Templates are somewhat controversial word processing tools. Templates provide the formatting, and often some of the text, for standard documents. They are available for letters, resumes, memoranda, reports, brochures, pleadings, theses, and other documents. Advocates claim that templates free people to concentrate on the content, instead of the format, of a document. Critics argue that memorable work requires an understanding of the work in its entirety, including how its parts are put together. Templates, they maintain, result in bland, uninspired, look-alike drivel. For what type of documents are templates appropriate? For what type of work are they unsuitable? Why? With the availability of templates, is it still necessary to learn conventional formats for letters, resumes, reports, and theses? Why or why not?

Investigating the World

1. Most word processing software offers similar features, but all word processing software is not the same. Menus, toolbars, layouts, fonts, and other features differ from one application to the next. Visit a software vendor and compare at least two types of word processing software (such as Word and WordPerfect). How are they similar? How are they different? Which one is easier to use? Why? Is either application compatible with (able to work with) any other applications? If so, which one(s)? What is the price of each application? Based on what you have learned and how you anticipate you would use a word processor, which software would you be more likely to purchase? Why?

2. In addition to complete word processing programs such as Word and WordPerfect, word processing software also is built into integrated packages such as Microsoft Works and ClarisWorks, and even included with some operating systems (for example, a word processing program called WordPad is included with Windows 95). Visit a software vendor and try a word processing program that is part of an integrated package or included with an operating system. With which application or operating system is the program associated? Which features described in this lab are included in the program? What features are not included? Is the program easy to use? Why or why not? What are the advantages and limitations of the software? Would you be happy with a word processing program that is included with an integrated package or an operating system, or would you prefer a complete word processing program? Why?

Working with Spreadsheets

Summarizing the Lab

4

Instructions: Use the *Working with Spreadsheets* interactive lab to complete the following outline.

I. What is a spreadsheet and spreadsheet software?

A _spreadsheet_ is a worksheet that resembles a table for organizing numbers.

Manual spreadsheets have been used for a long time to manage and keep track of data. Spreadsheet software can perform these same operations and many more in a spreadsheet file that may contain as many as 255 spreadsheets.

The first electronic spreadsheet, VisiCalc, was introduced in 1979.

II. Spreadsheet files

Electronic spreadsheets have the distinguishing features shown in Figure 4 on the next page.

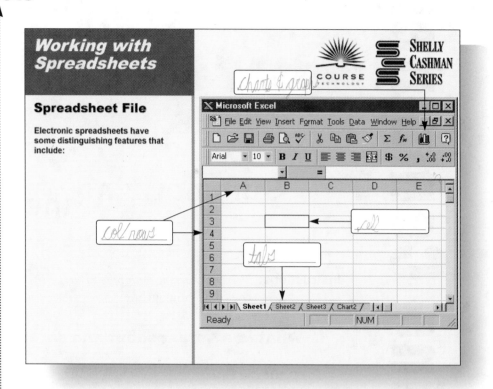

Figure 4

A. _Tabs_ typically are on the bottom frame of the window and can be customized with a label describing each spreadsheet. The order of the tab sheets can be arranged so that those frequently used can be grouped together.

A spreadsheet file usually contains several related tab sheets. For example, tab sheets labeled Income, Expenses, Payroll, Profit, Growth, and so on, may all be part of a company's Quarterly Performance spreadsheet file.

B. Each spreadsheet has 256 _columns_ and 65,356 _rows_.

Columns are identified by letters ranging from A to IV. Rows are designated with numbers from 1 to 65,356.

Only a small fraction of a spreadsheet displays on the screen.

Scroll bars, scroll arrows, and scroll boxes on the bottom and the right side of the window can be used to view different parts of a spreadsheet.

C. _Cells_ are where rows and columns meet and are identified with a column letter and row number.

This identification is called a cell address or cell reference. The column letter in a cell reference can be uppercase or lowercase, but it always appears first. The column letter and row number must be adjacent with no spaces between.

The cell address for the cell at the intersection of column D and row 5 is _____.

A spreadsheet has more than 16,000,000 cells. When a cell is selected (clicked), a heavy border surrounds the cell and the cell reference displays in a Name box above and to the left of the spreadsheet window. Data entered in the cell appears to the right of the Name box in what is called the *formula bar*.

A range is a series of adjacent cells. A range is selected by dragging. Ranges are designated with the beginning cell reference, a punctuation mark (such as a colon), and then the ending cell reference (for example, C5:F5 is the range of cells in row 5 from column C to column F).

Exploring Online

The Web is a great resource for information on spreadsheets. The Spreadsheet Tools and Standards page, for example, provides recommendations on basic spreadsheet design, while The Spreadsheet Page includes tips, templates, and links to online tutorials for Microsoft Excel, Lotus 1-2-3, and Corel Quattro Pro. The Web sites of Microsoft, Lotus, and Corel also provide extensive information on their specific spreadsheet software. For more information on working with spreadsheets, visit the Exploring Computers Web page (www.scsite.com/expl.htm) and click Spreadsheets.

III. Cells

Three types of data or information can be input into a cell:

- *text or labels*
- *Numbers or values*
- *Formulas or instructions*

Inputting text, then numbers, and finally formulas is a useful order for entering data.

A. *Text or labels* usually are the first thing added to a spreadsheet.

Labels help identify the data and organize the spreadsheet. Labels should be descriptive to make data input easier.

In most spreadsheet programs, cells are eight to ten characters wide. If text is longer than the width of the cell, the text flows into the adjacent cell on the right when the adjacent cell is empty. Cell width can be adjusted using a feature known as AutoFit or by dragging the column boundary to the right or left.

The _enter_ key completes an entry. Depending on how the spreadsheet program is set up, when the **ENTER** key is pressed the cell may remain selected or the selection may move to an adjacent cell. With some spreadsheet programs, an entry also can be completed by pressing the **TAB** key or an arrow key or by clicking the Enter box (check mark) in the formula bar.

B. After the text is entered, the next step is to input the _numbers_ or data.

Some spreadsheet programs allow a cell to be *protected* when it contains data that should not change. Protecting a cell prevents it from being altered accidentally. The cell's contents cannot be changed until the protection is removed.

C. Formulas perform calculations and display the resulting values.

auto Sum adds the values in selected cells and places the total in the last selected cell.

In most spreadsheet programs, formulas are preceded by a symbol, such as = or @, to distinguish them from text.

Formulas can be copied from one cell and pasted into another cell using the Copy and Paste buttons on the toolbar or the Copy and Paste commands on the Edit menu. When a cell is copied, its contents are placed in a temporary storage location called the Clipboard. A moving border, often called a marquee, surrounds the copied cell.

When a formula is pasted, the cell references are updated automatically (changed to fit the new location). This automatic updating is called _relative addressing_.

Cell references can be kept constant (unchanged) by placing a dollar sign in front of the column letter and row number. When the cell reference, D5, appears in a formula, the cell reference is *not* updated. The value in cell D5 is used whenever the formula is calculated, even if the formula is copied to a new location. This is called absolute referencing. When only the column is kept constant (as in $D5), only the row is kept constant (as in D$5), or neither the row nor the column is kept constant (as in D5), it is called relative referencing.

D. The _percent_ button is used to format a number as a percent.

Other toolbar buttons also can be used to format numbers. The Currency Style button formats numbers as dollar amounts. The Comma Style button formats numbers with commas between periods. The Increase Decimal and Decrease Decimal buttons increase or decrease the number of digits displayed after the decimal point.

Exploring Windows 95

Many spreadsheet applications are available in versions designed to take advantage of the features of Windows 95. Some of these spreadsheets include:

- Corel Quattro Pro
- Lotus 1-2-3
- Microsoft Excel

Files created in one of the spreadsheet applications listed above usually can be saved in a specific format so they can be read by one of the other spreadsheets.

IV. Changing data in a spreadsheet

With a manual spreadsheet, when one value changes, all related values must be manually recalculated. When data in an electronic spreadsheet is changed, formulas are recalculated automatically and new values are generated.

A. The capability to automatically recalculate is called *what-if-analysis*

Because what-if analysis allows users to see the results of changing data in a spreadsheet, it is a powerful decision-making tool.

Another decision-making tool provided by most spreadsheet software is called goal seeking. Goal seeking determines the input value necessary for a formula to achieve a desired result or goal.

B. Many spreadsheet programs come with built-in formulas called *Functions*.

Some spreadsheet programs have more than 200 built-in functions. These functions are separated into several categories such as:

- *Financial*
- *Statistical*
- *Text*
- *Date & Time*
- *Lookup (searching)& Reference*
- *Logical*
- *Math & Trigonometry*
- *Database*
- *Cell, Col. & Row information*

C. *Help* gives a description of circumstances when and how a function would be used.

Exploring Your Computer

Create one of these simple manual spreadsheets on paper:

- A school budget spreadsheet, with rows for expenses such as tuition, books, lab fees, club dues, and supplies. Provide data for two different quarters or semesters and add up the total expenses.

- A win-loss record spreadsheet, with rows for team names and columns for wins, losses, and ties. Find the total wins, losses, and ties for the league, as well as the total number of games played.

If you have access to a spreadsheet program, such as Excel, Quattro Pro, or Lotus 1-2-3, create an electronic version of your spreadsheet, entering data in at least four different rows or columns.

V. Graphs and charts

In addition to making numerical calculations very quickly, the results can be turned into charts and graphs that graphically show relationships.

Charts and graphs put numerical relationships in a more concrete form so they can be recognized more quickly and be understood easily.

The charts and graphs available with spreadsheet applications are called _analytical or_ _Business graphics_ because they are used in making business decisions.

There are several different types of graphs. When selecting a graph type, it is important to choose the one that best portrays the data. The three most common graph types are:

- Line charts — to represent a trend over time

- Bar charts — to show relationships among data

- Pie charts — to illustrate relationships of parts to a whole

Other graph types include scatter charts, area charts, doughnut charts, and radar charts.

Evaluating the **Results**

True/False

Instructions: Circle **T** if the statement is true or **F** if the statement is false.

(T) **F** 1. A spreadsheet file can contain as many as 255 spreadsheets.

T (F) 2. Each spreadsheet has 65,356 columns and 256 rows.

T (F) 3. Text or labels usually are the last thing added to a spreadsheet.

(T) **F** 4. Labels should be descriptive to make it easier to input data.

(T) **F** 5. When data is changed in a spreadsheet, formulas are recalculated automatically and new values are generated.

Matching

Instructions: Write the letter of a description from the column on the right in front of each term in the column on the left.

___e__ 1. Tab sheets

___a__ 2. Columns and rows

___d__ 3. Cells

___c__ 4. Charts and tables

___g__ 5. Functions

a. organize data vertically and horizontally

b. feature that automatically adjusts column width

c. illustrate relationships among data

d. where columns and rows meet

e. typically at the bottom of a window

f. below and to the right of a spreadsheet window

g. built-in formulas

Multiple Choice

Instructions: Circle the correct response.

1. Which of the following can be used to view different parts of a spreadsheet?
   a. scroll bars
   b. scroll arrows
   c. scroll boxes
   d. all of the above

2. Where is cell D5 located?
   a. on tab sheet D in row 5
   b. at the intersection of column D and row 5
   c. on tab sheet D in column 5
   d. at the intersection of column 5 and row D

3. Which key should be pressed after inputting each number in a spreadsheet?
   a. **ENTER**
   b. **SPACEBAR**
   c. **END**
   d. **INSERT**

4. What is the capability to automatically recalculate formulas when values are changed?
   a. relative referencing
   b. AutoFit
   c. what-if analysis
   d. cell addressing

5. What are analytical graphics?
   a. charts and graphs used in making business decisions
   b. text used to identify data
   c. built-in formulas that are broken up into several categories
   d. multiple series of adjacent cells

Fill in the Blanks

Instructions: Place the correct word(s) in the blank in each sentence.

1. A(n) _spreadsheet_ is a worksheet that resembles a table for organizing numbers.

2. Data entered into a cell displays to the right of the Name box in what is called the _formula bar_ .

3. _Autosum_ adds the values in selected cells and places the total in the last selected cell.

4. The updating of cell references when a formula is pasted into another cell is called _relative referencing_

5. Some spreadsheet applications have a program called _help_ that describes how to use many of the features available.

Examining the Issues

1. Designing a successful spreadsheet can be a daunting task. Good spreadsheets not only produce correct results, they also help users understand those results. The following guidelines have been offered for designing effective spreadsheets:

   - Use specific titles and documentation

   - Date spreadsheets internally

   - List any assumptions made

   - List or print formulas

   - Check input values with an IF function

   - Check computations with values that have known results

   Why is each guideline important? What other practices can help make spreadsheets more effective? How?

2. Many business decisions involve risk. In a process called risk analysis, managers use spreadsheets to weigh the degree of risk. Various outcomes (returns) are suggested, a probability is assigned to each outcome, expected values are computed, and then the expected values are totaled. For example, a manager considering investing in FlimFlams or JibJabs may perform the following risk analysis:

Possible Return	Probability (FlimFlams)	Probability (JibJabs)	Expected Value (FlimFlams)	Expected Value (JibJabs)
$50,000	30%	50%	50,000 x .30 = 15,000	50,000 x .50 = 25,000
$10,000	60%	20%	10,000 x .60 = 6,000	10,000 x .20 = 2,000
$0	10%	30%	0 x .10 = 0	0 x .30 = 0
Total Expected Values			$21,000	$27,000

   Based on this risk analysis, in which product would a manager invest? Why? What other factors may influence a manager's decision? What risks are involved in risk analysis?

Investigating the World

1. Recent surveys show that word processing software and spreadsheet applications are the most used productivity applications. In addition to recording income and expenses, spreadsheet programs have assumed a wide range of other functions. A medical center that treats accident victims also supplies spreadsheets estimating the types, frequency, and costs of treatments for insurance purposes. A noted restaurant uses spreadsheet software to inventory its wine cellar, determining the popularity of each vintage and reducing what once was a two-day chore to a one-hour task. Visit a local business and interview someone familiar with how the company uses spreadsheet software. What application is used? Why? For what purposes are spreadsheets used? How has the use of spreadsheets benefited the company? What problems are associated with using spreadsheets?

2. In 1983, an innovative program developed by Mitch Kapor revealed the far-reaching capabilities of spreadsheet software. Kapor, a teacher of transcendental meditation, called his program Lotus 1-2-3 because it combined three elements (spreadsheets, graphics, and databases) in a spreadsheet program that was "as easy as one, two, three" to use. Lotus 1-2-3 dominated the spreadsheet market until 1991 when Microsoft released Excel 2, which was designed to take advantage of the Windows environment. Excel surged to the front of the market with features such as 3-dimensional graphics, auxiliary functions, wizards to guide users through complex tasks, powerful what-if tools, and easy-to-use database capabilities. Today, other spreadsheet programs, such as Corel Quattro Pro, have joined Lotus 1-2-3 and Excel. Visit a software vendor and compare two or more spreadsheet applications. How are they similar? How are they different? What is the cost of each? With what other applications are they compatible? Based on your comparison, which software would you recommend? Why?

Understanding the Motherboard

Summarizing the Lab

5

Instructions: Use the *Understanding the Motherboard* interactive lab to complete the following outline.

I. What is a motherboard?

Computer program instructions are executed and data is manipulated in the system unit. A motherboard, sometimes called the main board or system board, is a _circuit board_ that contains most of the electronic components of the system unit.

II. Components of a motherboard

The components on a PC's motherboard are illustrated in Figure 5 on the next page.

A. The _CPU_ contains the control unit and the arithmetic/logic unit.

- The control unit can be thought of as the *brain* of the computer. It operates by repeatedly fetching program instructions from memory, decoding program instructions into commands the computer can process, executing the computer commands, and then storing the results of the instructions in memory. This process is called the machine cycle.

- The arithmetic/logic unit (ALU) contains the electronic circuitry necessary to perform arithmetic and logical operations on data. Arithmetic operations include addition, subtraction, multiplication, and division. Logical operations consist of comparing one data item to another. Based on the result of the comparison, different types of processing may occur.

B. _Read Only Memory (ROM)_ chips contain a permanent set of instructions called BIOS (Basic Input/Output System) that provides the interface between the operating system and hardware devices.

Understanding the Motherboard

COURSE TECHNOLOGY

SHELLY CASHMAN SERIES

Components of a motherboard

On the motherboard of a PC, you will find:

RAM

expansion *slots*

keyboard connector

Serial Port

CPU *Socket*

ROM

Parallel Port

disk drive *conector*

Figure 5

Many of the special-purpose computers used in automobiles, appliances, and so on, use small amounts of ROM to store repeatedly executed instructions.

C. *Random Access Memory (RAM)* is the name given to the chips that are used for memory.

Memory stores three items:

- *The operating system*
- *Application programs*
- *Data*

Data and programs are transferred into and out of RAM, and data stored in RAM is manipulated by computer program instructions.

D. *Expansion Slots* are where additional add-on peripheral devices are attached to the motherboard.

E. The *keyboard connector* is where the keyboard is connected to the motherboard.

F. The *serial port* transmits data one bit at a time.

A bit (short for binary digit) can represent one of two values: on or off. Cables connecting serial ports generate little electrical interference and can be up to 1,000 feet long. Devices such as modems usually are connected to a serial port.

G. A *Parallel port* transmits data eight bits, called a byte, at a time.

A byte can represent 256 different data possibilities. Although faster than a serial port, electrical signals in a parallel cable tend to interfere with one another over long distances, so parallel cables usually are limited to 50 feet. Printers or tape backup devices usually are connected to a parallel port.

H. The _disk drive connector_ is where the hard disk is connected to the motherboard.

Each connector is designed so it can fit in only one type of socket and in only one correct position.

I. The _System Bus_ is the circuitry that connects all of the motherboard components together so they can communicate.

Exploring Online

Intel Corporation is the primary manufacturer of processors for personal computers. Intel's Web site has information on processors Intel currently produces and future products that are under development. Two of Intel's major competitors are Cyrix and Advanced Micro Devices. To learn more about the latest processors and other components of the motherboard, visit the Exploring Computers Web page (www.scsite.com/expl.htm) and click Motherboard.

III. CPU choices

A. CPUs for PCs are available in several different classes: _8088_ , _8\286_ , _386_ (SX or DX), _486_ (SX or DX), and _pentium_ .

B. Processor speed is measured by _megahertz_ , which means millions of cycles per second.

Speed is determined by the system clock, which generates electronic pulses at a fixed rate and is used by the control unit to synchronize all computer operations.

C. A more advanced CPU executing instructions at the same speed as an older one is still more productive because it needs fewer instructions to accomplish the same amount of work.

CPUs using CISC (complex instruction set computing) technology have hundreds of commands in their instruction sets. RISC (reduced instruction set computing) technology reduces the instructions to only those used most frequently. This increases the CPU's overall processing capability.

D. Some processor names end with SX or DX. An _SX_ processor is less powerful than a _DX_ processor of the same type.

E. _Pentium_ and _Pentium Pro_ chips are very powerful processors available for the PC. Each of these chips has a built-in math coprocessor, or _FPU_, which is needed to help handle advanced mathematical calculations.

The _Pentium_ chip can execute over 100 million instructions per second, while the even more powerful _Pentium Pro_ chip can execute over 200 million instructions per second.

Exploring Windows 95

For optimal performance, Windows 95 requires greater capabilities than Windows 3.1. Microsoft recommends a 386 DX or higher processor, 4 megabytes of random access memory (RAM), and a VGA or higher resolution graphics card.

IV. ROM

A. ROM (read only memory) chips store information or instructions that do not change. ROM is described as _non-volatile_ because it retains its contents even when the power is turned off.

Data or programs stored in ROM can be read and used but cannot be altered, hence the name _read only memory_.

B. The _BIOS_ is the program stored in ROM that starts, or _boots,_ the system when it is first turned on, or _reboots_ it later if the computer must be restarted.

Instructions stored in ROM are called firmware or microcode.

V. RAM

A. RAM (random access memory) is the name given to chips that store programs and data that can change. RAM is described as _volatile_ because the programs and data in RAM are erased when the power to the computer is turned off.

The size of memory (RAM) is measured in kilobytes (K or KB) — approximately 1,000 bytes, or megabytes (MB) — approximately one million bytes.

B. Most modern systems use memory packages called _SIMM's_ or _Single In Line Memory Modules_. They are available in a variety of speeds, ranging from 50 to 100 nanoseconds (billionths of a second), and hold 1 to 64 megabytes each. They are installed two at a time.

Some computers improve their processing efficiency by using a limited amount of high-speed RAM, called cache memory, between the CPU and memory to store the most frequently used instructions and data.

Memory on personal computers can be divided into several areas: (a) conventional memory, which is used for the operating system, programs, and data; (b) upper memory, which is used for programs that control input and output devices and other computer hardware; and (c) extended memory, which consists of all memory above 1 MB and is used for programs and data. Older systems that cannot directly access more than 1 MB of memory use expanded memory on a memory expansion board.

VI. The internal bus: the data highway

A. A set of lines running between all the components on the motherboard, called the _internal bus_, provides the path for data transportation.

Sometimes these paths are actual wires, and sometimes they are etched lines on the circuit board or within the CPU.

B. Only _Two_ devices may use the bus at one time.

C. Buses can transfer multiples of eight bits at a time. Components have _8, 16, or 32_ lines connected to the bus.

VII. The expansion slots: the external bus

A. The _ext. bus_ is a row of slots at one end of the bus that allows the system to be expanded. Connecting circuit boards to slots adds capabilities to the computer system.

The circuit boards are called expansion boards (or sometimes expansion cards, controller cards, adapter cards, or interface cards). An expansion board usually is connected to the device it controls by a cable, and the expansion slot is connected to the expansion bus that transmits data to memory or the CPU.

B. Several different types of expansion slots exist:

1. _ISA_, found in older systems, have a narrow data path, so less information can travel along it at any given time.

2. _EISA_ and _VESA_ have twice as many lines, so twice as much data can be sent or received.

3. Newer systems add a _PCI_, with direct lines to the CPU for rapid transport.

Exploring Your Computer

What type of processor (286, 386, 486, Pentium, or Pentium Pro) is in your computer? How much random access memory (RAM) does your computer have? Are any peripheral devices, such as a sound card or modem, attached to your computer through the motherboard's expansion slots?

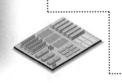

Evaluating the Results

True/False

Instructions: Circle **T** if the statement is true or **F** if the statement is false.

T F 1. The two components of the CPU work together using the program stored in memory (RAM) to perform the processing operations.

T F 2. If a processor can execute one instruction every cycle, with a 90 MHz processor it executes 90 million instructions every second.

T **F** 3. A DX processor is less powerful than an SX processor of the same type.

T **F** 4. ROM is described as volatile because the programs and data in ROM are erased when the power to the computer is turned off.

T **F** 5. All SIMMs installed on the motherboard must have different capacities.

Matching

Instructions: Write the letter of a description from the column on the right in front of each term in the column on the left.

_c_ 1. CPU

_a_ 2. Serial port

_e_ 3. Parallel port

_f_ 4. FPU

_g_ 5. Expansion slot

a. usually is connected to a modem

b. is the name given to chips that store information or instructions that do not change

c. executes program instructions and completes any arithmetic or logic operations

d. is a line running between all the components on the motherboard

e. usually is connected to a printer or tape backup

f. is a math coprocessor needed with older CPUs to handle advanced mathematical calculations

g. is used to add capabilities to a computer, such as high-resolution graphics, sound, and communications ports

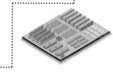

Multiple Choice

Instructions: Circle the correct response.

1. What is *not* stored in memory?
   a. the program that starts, or boots, the system when you first turn it on
   b. the application program that tells the computer what to do
   c. the data being manipulated
   d. the operating system that directs and coordinates the computer

2. All other components on the motherboard are designed to service which of the following?
   a. the keyboard connector
   b. the CPU
   c. the expansion slots
   d. the disk drive connector

3. What processor chip currently is the most powerful available for the PC?
   a. 80486SX
   b. 80486DX
   c. Pentium
   d. Pentium Pro

4. In addition to the program that starts, or boots, the computer system, what else is stored by the BIOS?
   a. information about the system's configuration
   b. the drivers that are installed
   c. the amount of memory available
   d. all of the above

5. What type of expansion slot is used for rapid transport in newer computer systems with direct lines to the CPU?
   a. SIMM
   b. ISA
   c. EISA
   d. PCI

Fill in the Blanks

Instructions: Place the correct word(s) in the blank in each sentence.

1. The _motherboard_, which contains most of the electronic components of the system unit, sits in the main housing along with the power supply.

2. The _CPU_ contains the control unit and the arithmetic/logic unit.

3. The _keyboard connector_ is where the set of keys used to enter data into a computer is joined to the motherboard.

4. The _system bus_ is the circuitry that connects all of the motherboard components so they can communicate with one another.

5. Processor speed is measured by _megahertz_, which means millions of cycles per second.

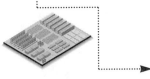

Examining the Issues

1. Consider the differences between ROM and RAM. In terms of your own memory, what kind of information do you have in your ROM memory? What kind of information do you have in your RAM memory? Why do you think special-purpose computers, such as those used in automobiles or appliances, use ROM instead of RAM?

2. ENIAC, the first computer, filled an entire room, yet it was less powerful than today's laptop computers. During the 1980s, the power of PCs expanded tenfold, and over the past twenty years the capacity of RAM has more than doubled every two years. As the processing power and memory of personal computers grow, it is becoming increasingly difficult to define *personal computer* and to separate it from its larger cousins. How do you define personal computer? Do you think your definition will still be valid twenty years from now? Why or why not?

Investigating the World

1. If you own or have access to a personal computer, unplug it and take the cover off the system unit. Make a sketch of the motherboard and try to identify as many components as you can. Be careful not to touch any of the components. Referring to the computer's *User Guide*, list the specifica-tions for some of the components described in this lab (for example, the CPU, CPU speed, bus speed, RAM type, RAM capacity, expansion slots, and so on).

2. Visit a computer vendor and compare one of its less expensive personal computer systems to one of its more expensive computer systems. Make a table that shows the differences between motherboard components (type of CPU, RAM capacity, and so on). Do you think the differences justify the discrepancy in price? Why or why not? Are there any other factors (such as included software) that may also affect the price disparity?

Scanning Documents

Summarizing the Lab

6

Instructions: Use the *Scanning Documents* interactive lab to complete the following outline.

I. What is a scanner?

A scanner is an input device that takes information on paper and converts it into *digital information* that can be used by a computer.

Most computers are digital and process data (text, sound, graphics, or video) that has been converted into a numeric (digital) value. The binary number system, which uses only the digits 0 and 1, is used to represent all values.

Inputting data with a scanner is a form of source data collection (or source data automation) because a scanner eliminates the manual entry of data. Source data collection can save time, minimize inputting errors, and help automate other parts of the processing cycle.

II. Types of scanning

The two types of scanning are *image scanning* and *scanning plus recognition*.

A. *Image scanning* creates a graphical representation of the page being scanned, electronically capturing the entire page of text or artwork.

The digital information collected by the scanner can be stored on disk, processed by a computer, and then printed or displayed separately or merged into another document such as a newsletter. This procedure, called image processing, has become widely used. As a result, image scanners play an increasingly important role in many offices.

B. _Scanning Plus Recognition_ attempts to find patterns in the scanned image and translate them into meaningful information.

Two common scanning processes that accomplish this are optical character recognition and bar code scanning.

1. _OCR_ results in data that can be processed by word processing software.

OCR is a specialized area — scanners that can read one type of symbol may not be able to read another. OCR devices range from hand-held wands to large machines that automatically read thousands of documents per minute. The standard OCR typeface, called OCR-A, can be read easily by both machines and people. OCR-B is a set of characters widely used in Europe and Japan. OCR technology is improving to include a wider assortment of characters, symbols, and even handwriting. OCR is used frequently for turn-around documents, such as billing statements, which are designed to be returned to the organization that created them.

OCR Software is used with image scanners to convert text images into data that can be used by word processing software. An entire page of text is scanned, and then the software attempts to identify individual words and letters.

OCR software usually is able to identify more than 98 percent of the scanned material. Any unidentified text is displayed for the operator to correct.

2. _Bar Code Scanners_ are designed to process bar codes, one type of optical code. A _Bar Code_ consists of a set of vertical lines, each of which represents either 1 or 0, and spaces. Every pattern of 1s, 0s, and spaces is associated with a specific _UPC Universal Product Code_ that identifies a product by name.

The UPC bar code, used for grocery and retail items, can be translated into a ten-digit number. This number is printed at the bottom of the bar code and can be input manually if the bar code

reader fails. Bar codes also are used by the postal service, shipping services, railroads, and book publishers. Hand-held guns, hand-held wands, or stationary readers can read bar codes.

Two other forms of scanning plus recognition are optical mark recognition (OMR) and magnetic ink character recognition (MICR). Optical mark recognition identifies the position of a mark and often is used to process standardized questionnaires or test answer sheets. Magnetic ink character recognition (MICR) is used by the banking industry to interpret characters that have been printed on the bottom of a check with a special magnetized ink. These characters indicate the bank, account number, check number, and the amount of the check after it has been cashed.

III. The image scanning process

Image scanning without OCR results only in a collection of _pixels_ that can be used by a software application.

Pixels, or picture elements, are the individual dots that can be illuminated to form an image on the computer screen.

Image scanning takes place using one of the three types of scanners shown in Figure 6.

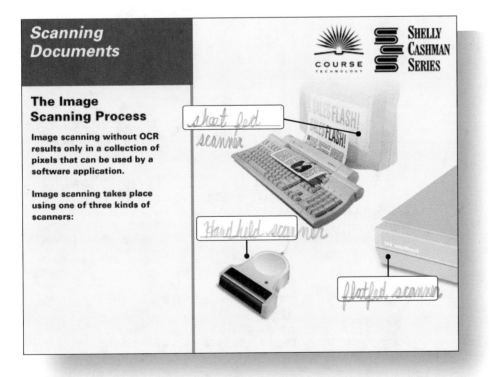

Scanning Documents

COURSE TECHNOLOGY

SHELLY CASHMAN SERIES

The Image Scanning Process

Image scanning without OCR results only in a collection of pixels that can be used by a software application.

Image scanning takes place using one of three kinds of scanners:

sheet fed scanner

Hand held scanner

flatbed scanner

Figure 6

A. A _flat bed scanner_ operates much like a copy machine.

1. A light source within the scanner illuminates the image located against the scanner's glass surface.

2. A _scan head_ moves along the page picking up reflected light and projecting it to pivoting mirrors, which then project it to a lens.

3. The lens focuses the light onto a _light sensitive diode_, which converts it into electrical current of different voltages that correspond to the brightness of the reflected light.

4. The current is sent to an _analog digital converter_, which changes the voltages into digital impulses.

5. The _digital impulses (zeros & ones)_ are sent to the computer to be used by different software applications.

Hand-held scanners are adequate for scanning small areas; however, because they depend on a steady hand, the overall quality can deteriorate when scanning large images.

Exploring Your Computer

Scanners usually are connected to computers through a SCSI (small computer standard interface). Other types of SCSI devices include CD-ROM drives and tape backup systems. Do you have a scanner, or any other type of SCSI device, attached to your computer?

B. Scanned images may be _Black and White_, _Gray scale_, or _Color_. The scanning process is slightly different for each.

1. When scanning in _Black & White_, the analog-to-digital converter stores the voltage readings as either black (1) or white (0).

2. Scanning images in _grayscale_ means that the voltage readings are stored as shades of gray, instead of only black and white.

   Images scanned in grayscale are like black and white photographs.

3. To scan images in _color_, the scan head makes three passes under the image. Each pass uses a different color filter (red, green, or blue) to modify the color of the light. The full-color image is made by combining the results of the three passes.

The cost of scanners, both hand-held and full-page, has decreased significantly during the past few years. Full-page color scanners are the most expensive. Color images require more storage space than black and white images of the same resolution.

C. The term _resolution_ refers to the number of pixels per square inch displayed on the screen.

The resolution, or clarity, of the image depends on the number of pixels and the distance between them. The greater the number of pixels and the closer they are, the better the resolution. Resolution is defined in _Dots Per Inch_ , or DPI.

1. The _lower_ the resolution at which an image is scanned, the lower the quality of the final image.

    Because they must be moved over an image by hand, the resolution of hand-held scanners is lower than the resolution of flatbed scanners.

    Low resolution images generally take up _less_ memory.

2. The _higher_ the resolution at which an image is scanned, the higher the quality of the final image.

    High resolution images can take up _a great deal_ of memory.

    High quality laser scanners are used by newspapers, publishers, and service bureaus because of their accuracy.

Exploring Windows 95

Windows 95 supports Plug-and-Play hardware devices. When a Plug-and-Play scanner is attached to a Windows 95 computer, Windows 95 automatically detects the scanner and installs the appropriate software, or drivers, to control it.

Evaluating the Results

True/False

Instructions: Circle **T** if the statement is true or **F** if the statement is false.

T F 1. Two common scanning processes that convert scanned input into more meaningful information are optical character recognition (OCR) and bar code scanning.

T **F** 2. The most commonly used scanner, the sheet-fed scanner, operates much like a copy machine.

T **F** 3. When the light source within a flatbed scanner illuminates the image, white portions of the page reflect less light than images or words.

T F 4. To create a full-color image, the scan head in a flatbed scanner makes three passes under the image.

T **F** 5. A low resolution image generally takes up a great deal of memory.

Matching

Instructions: Write the letter of a description from the column on the right in front of each term in the column on the left.

_a_ 1. Scanning

_d_ 2. Image scanning

_f_ 3. Scanning plus recognition

_e_ 4. Bar code scanning

_b_ 5. Black and white scanning

a. takes information on paper and converts it into digital form

b. employs an analog-to-digital converter that stores voltage readings as either 1 or 0

c. identifies the position of a mark made on a standardized form

d. creates a graphical representation of the image scanned and electronically captures an entire page

e. processes a type of optical code consisting of vertical lines and spaces

f. attempts to find patterns in a scanned image and translate them into meaningful information

g. combines three different scan passes to create an image

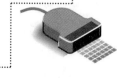

Multiple Choice

Instructions: Circle the correct response.

1. What are the two types of scanning?
   a. optical character recognition (OCR) and bar code scanning
   b. black and white scanning and color scanning
   c. image scanning and scanning plus recognition
   d. hand-held scanning and sheet-fed scanning

2. What is used with image scanners to convert text images into data that can be processed by word processing software?
   a. OCR software
   b. RBG software
   c. UPC software
   d. OMR software

3. Which of the following is *not* a scanner used for image scanning?
   a. sheet-fed scanner
   b. bar code scanner
   c. hand-held scanner
   d. flatbed scanner

4. In a flatbed scanner, what converts light focused by the lens into electrical current containing different voltages?
   a. a scan head
   b. a pivoting mirror
   c. an analog-digital converter
   d. a light-sensitive diode

5. When capturing an image in color, which of the following is *not* one of the color filters used to modify the color of light directed at the image?
   a. red
   b. yellow
   c. blue
   d. green

Fill in the Blanks

Instructions: Place the correct word(s) in the blank in each sentence.

1. _OCR_____ results in data that can be processed by word processing software.

2. A(n) _bar code_____ consists of a set of vertical lines and spaces.

3. Each pattern of 1s and 0s processed by a bar code scanner in a store is associated with an _UPC_____ that identifies the product by name.

4. Some scanners scan images in _grayscale_____, which means the voltage readings are stored as shades of gray, instead of only black or white.

5. The term _resolution_____ refers to the number of pixels per square inch displayed on the screen.

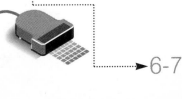

Examining the Issues

1. Using an image scanner and a computer, a photograph can be altered subtly to create a desired effect. The cover of a news magazine once showed a photograph of a famous person who had been accused of a grisly crime. The photograph had been retouched to give the figure a more sinister appearance. Some people objected to the cover, claiming that it implied the defendant was guilty even before he had been tried. Others insisted, however, that the photograph was not offered as an exact representation but as a graphic portrayal of the seriousness of the accusation. Under what circumstances, if any, is it appropriate to enhance a photograph using a computer? What can be done to prevent retouched photographs from being accepted as literal truth?

2. To produce accurate information, a computer requires accurate input. Inaccurate information caused by inaccurate data can be worse than no information at all. The need for accurate input is summarized by the computer jargon term GIGO, which stands for *Garbage In, Garbage Out*. Of the three input devices described in these labs (the mouse, the keyboard, and scanners), which is most likely to result in accurate input? Why? Which is least likely to result in accurate input? Why? What factors have the greatest influence on input accuracy?

Investigating the World

1. The cost of scanners has decreased significantly during the past few years. Visit a computer vendor and examine the scanners available. What type of scanner (hand-held, sheet-fed, or flatbed; black-and-white, grayscale, or color) is least expensive? Why? What type of scanner is most expensive? Why? For what purposes would the most inexpensive scanner be adequate? When would the most expensive scanner be required? If you were purchasing a scanner for yourself, which type would you buy? Why?

2. Bar code scanners are used by retail stores, supermarkets, and libraries. Visit an organization that uses bar code scanners and interview a manager to find out how the scanners are used. What kind of information is the organization able to collect? How is the information used? In what ways does the information obtained through the use of scanners benefit the organization or the organization's clientele? Was the organization able to keep track of the same information before it used scanners? Why or why not?

Setting Up to Print

Summarizing the Lab

7

Instructions: Use the *Setting Up to Print* interactive lab to complete the following outline.

I. Printing: the computer revolution

Low-cost, high-quality printers help computer users create professional quality documents.

Output that is printed is called hard copy. Printing requirements differ greatly, and as a result, printers have been developed with varying speeds, capabilities, and printing methods.

Hardware and *software* components work together to change electronic documents into a printed page.

II. Printer choices

Printers fall into the two categories illustrated in Figure 7 on the next page.

A. *Impact* printers are inexpensive and can print on continuous forms, but they can be noisy.

Front striking impact printers strike the mechanism that forms the character against an inked ribbon, which in turn strikes the front of the paper (similar to a typewriter). Hammer striking impact printers strike a hammer against the back of the paper, pushing the paper against an inked ribbon and the desired character. Most impact printers use continuous-form paper composed of sheets connected together for a continuous flow through the printer.

Dot Matrix printers are examples of impact printers.

Dot matrix printers produce images by striking wire pins against an inked ribbon. The combination of small dots forms a character, much like the characters produced by combinations of light bulbs on an electronic scoreboard. Draft-quality printing uses the minimum

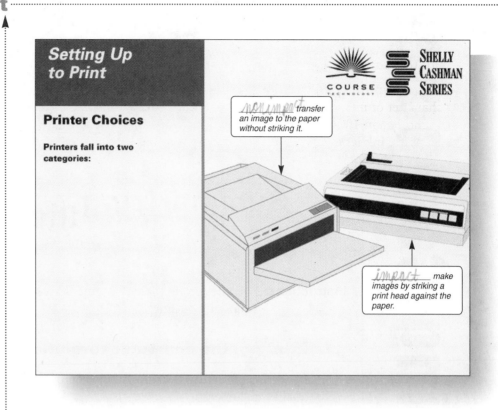

Figure 7

number of dots to form a character. Letter quality (LQ) and near letter quality (NLQ) printing, in which a higher-quality look is achieved by overlapping dots, is done at slower speeds. Most dot matrix printers have moveable print heads and are designed to print in a bidirectional manner (that is, from left to right and then back again from right to left). The speed of impact printers with moveable print heads is measured in characters per second or cps.

Band and chain printers, which print using a rotating band or chain, are impact printers used for high-volume output on large computer systems. These printers print an entire line at a time.

B. _Nonimpact_ printers output at a much higher resolution than impact printers and are nearly silent.

Nonimpact printers use chemicals, laser light, or heat to transfer an image to paper. The resolution of most nonimpact printers is from 300 to 720 dpi (dots per inch). The resolution of a dot matrix printer is typically less than 100 dpi. The speed of nonimpact printers is measured in pages per minute or ppm. The majority of nonimpact printers use individual sheets of paper stored in a removable tray that slides into the printer case.

The most common types of nonimpact printers are the _Ink Jet/Bubble Jet_ printer and the _Laser_ printer.

Ink jet printers spray tiny drops of ink onto the paper to form a character or image. Because the print nozzle can contain from 50 to more than 100 small holes, they produce high-quality print or graphics. Ink jet printers are quiet and print at rates of 30 to 150 cps. Ink jet printers require good quality, single-sheet paper to prevent the ink from bleeding.

A third type of nonimpact printers, called thermal printers or thermal transfer printers, uses heat to transfer colored inks from ink sheets onto the printing surface.

Exploring Online

Major suppliers of computer printers include Hewlett-Packard, Epson, and Canon. To learn more about these companies and the different types of printers they offer, visit the Exploring Computers Web page (www.scsite.com/expl.htm) and click Printers.

C. How a laser printer works

1. A laser beam converts data from the computer into _pulses of light_

2. A _revolving mirror_ reflects the light against the surface of a photosensitive drum.

3. Areas of the drum touched by the reflected laser beam pick up an _electrostatic charge_ which attracts _toner particles_ that collect on the drum.

4. As a sheet of paper is fed past the rotating drum, the drum transfers the toner pattern to the paper using _heat_ and _pressure_ .

Laser printers used with personal computers range in speed from 4 to 12 pages per minute (ppm). Laser printers usually come with a large number of built-in fonts, or character sets. Laser printers used with individual personal computers start at less than $300. They represent the fastest growing segment of the printer market.

III. Connecting the printer

The printer is connected to the computer using a _parallel cable_ , which contains eight lines for data along with other lines for grounding and synchronization.

The electrical signals in a parallel cable tend to interfere with one another over a long distance, so parallel cables usually are limited to 50 feet. Personal computer parallel cables are usually six to ten feet long.

Most PCs communicate to the printer using the _parallel port_, which is referenced as _LPT1_. This port can send eight bits, or a single byte, to the printer at one time.

Parallel ports are used most often to connect devices that send or receive large amounts of data.

> ### Exploring Your Computer
>
> Is there a printer attached to your computer? Is it attached directly to the computer through a parallel port or is it connected via a network? Is your printer an impact or nonimpact printer? What brand of printer is it?

IV. Setting up communications

Attaching a printer to a computer system involves configuring the computer so that it knows the capabilities of the printer and is able to communicate with it.

A. A _printer driver_ is a program that converts the computer's printing instructions into commands the printer can understand.

In order for a printer to function, an appropriate printer driver must be installed on the computer. Most printer manufacturers include driver software with their printers; many operating systems also include printer drivers.

B. Communicating with the printer

The computer can communicate with the printer in two ways:

1. High-resolution page information can be fed line by line to a variety of printers without internal processing capabilities using the printer's _low level commands_.

2. A _page description language_ enables the computer to describe elements of the page individually to printers that have internal processing capabilities, such as laser printers.

Using a page description language allows a document created on one computer to be printed on another computer with a different printer, as long as the second printer has a compatible page description language.

V. Preparing documents

A. Print setup features, which control the way documents are printed, are set using the Print dialog box in _Most_ application programs, such as Microsoft Word 97.

B. The _Print_ dialog box presents basic options, such as paper orientation.

Portrait orientation means the paper is taller than it is wide. This is the orientation used for most correspondence. Landscape orientation means the paper is wider than it is tall. This orientation often is used for tables with a large number of columns.

C. The _Graphics_ tab in the Properties dialog box can be used to add special effects, such as reversing or mirroring the image.

VI. Printing text

Fonts are files that are used by a computer's operating system to display text in different styles.

Fonts are a combination of typeface (character sets such as Times Roman, with a specific appearance and shape) and point size (the height of the type; each point is approximately 1/72 of an inch). Often, two different files exist for each font: a bitmap version and an outline version. TrueType fonts require only a single file.

A. _Bit Map font_, also called screen fonts, are pixel-based fonts designed to display on the screen the way the printed page will look.

In bitmap fonts, each pixel (which equals a bit) is illuminated individually by a combination of graphics hardware and software.

B. _High resolution_ _outline fonts_, which describe, or trace, the typeface using curves and angles, are used for printing. This enables the printer to print the font in any size.

C. _True Type_ fonts are a kind of outline font that is designed also to be used on the screen.

TrueType fonts appear in the printed document the same as they appear on the screen, which is important in applications such as desktop publishing. In Windows applications, the names of TrueType fonts are preceded by **T̲T̲**. TrueType fonts are included with Windows 95.

VII. Using fonts

A. When text is emphasized by making it _italic_ or **bold**, it is called changing the _style_ of the text.

A style is a customized format applied to characters. Underlining is another style.

B. When the computer sends an outline font that is not in the printer along with the document, it is called *down loading* the font.

The downloaded font is stored in the printer's memory while the document is printing.

Because most printers are 1,000 times slower than computers, they have a buffer that temporarily stores information, allowing the computer to dump output into the buffer and continue processing.

Exploring Windows 95

Windows 95 allows users to drag and drop graphical representations of files to perform certain functions. For example, a word processing document can be printed by dragging the icon representing the document to a printer icon and then dropping it.

VIII. Printing grayscale images

Black-and-white printers reproduce grayscale images using a *fine pattern of dots*, which appear as shades of gray when viewed at a distance.

A. *Dithering*, a technique generally used by impact printers, is creating a shade of gray by printing dots of the same size and varying their number.

B. *Halftoning*, which can be done using nonimpact printers to give a more realistic effect, is creating a shade of gray by printing a regular pattern of dots and varying their size. Newspapers often use this technique to reproduce photographs.

IX. Printing color images

Color documents are printed by making multiple passes over the paper using *primary colors*, which are mixed on the page to produce the desired hue.

Color output is more attractive, but it is slower and more expensive for all printer types.

Evaluating the Results

True/False

Instructions: Circle **T** if the statement is true or **F** if the statement is false.

T (F) 1. Impact printers produce output with much higher resolution than nonimpact printers and are nearly silent.

(T) **F** 2. The printer is connected to the computer using a parallel cable, which contains eight lines for data along with other lines for grounding and synchronization.

T (F) 3. Most PCs communicate with the printer using the serial port.

(T) **F** 4. Often, two different files exist for each font: a bitmap or pixel-based version and an outline version that describes the characters using curves and angles.

(T) **F** 5. Color documents are printed by making multiple passes over the paper using primary colors and mixing the colors on the page to produce the desired hue.

Matching

Instructions: Write the letter of a description from the column on the right in front of each term in the column on the left.

___d___ 1. Printer driver

___c___ 2. Low level printer command

___g___ 3. Page description language

___e___ 4. Dithering

___a___ 5. Halftoning

a. is used by newspapers to reproduce photographs and can be done with nonimpact printers

b. presents specialized print options, such as changing the intensity and detail of the image

c. feeds high resolution page information to a printer without internal processing capabilities

d. configures the computer so it knows the capabilities of the printer

e. is used by impact printers because they can print only dots of a single size

f. is capable of sending eight bits, or a single byte, to the printer at one time

g. enables a computer to specify elements of a page individually

Multiple Choice

Instructions: Circle the correct response.

1. Which of the following is a type of impact printer?
   a. dot matrix printer
   b. laser printer
   c. ink jet printer
   d. all of the above

2. In a laser printer, the laser beam converts data from the computer into what?
   a. grayscale images
   b. bitmap fonts
   c. pulses of light
   d. toner particles

3. How is the parallel port referenced in a PC system?
   a. LPT1
   b. MIDI
   c. COM1
   d. RJ-11

4. For Windows applications, what window is used to set basic options such as what printer to use, in what orientation to print, and the size and source of the paper?
   a. Page Description dialog box
   b. Print Setup dialog box
   c. Print dialog box
   d. Advanced Options dialog box

5. What kind of fonts, included with the Windows 95 operating system, are designed to look the same when they are printed as they appear on the screen?
   a. bitmap fonts
   b. screen fonts
   c. TrueType fonts
   d. outline fonts

Fill in the Blanks

Instructions: Place the correct word(s) in the blank in each sentence.

1. _Impact_ printers make images by striking a print head against the paper.

2. _Nonimpact_ printers transfer an image to the screen without striking it.

3. A(n) _print driver_ is a program that converts the computer's printing instructions into commands the printer can understand.

4. _Fonts_ are files that are used by a computer's operating system to display text in different styles.

5. When the computer sends an outline font to the printer along with the document, it is called _down loading_ the font.

Examining the Issues

1. An office secretary recently expressed anxiety about the future. Low-cost, high-quality printers, powerful personal computers, and easy-to-use software have had a substantial impact on the office environment. Company executives who once had secretaries prepare all their reports and correspondence now are creating, editing, and revising their own documents. Is there still a place for the secretary in the modern office? Are the secretary's fears justified? Why or why not? How will the computer revolution affect traditional jobs?

2. When computers first were used in business, many people envisioned the *paperless office* — a place where most documents would exist only electronically as a computer file. Yet surprisingly, many offices actually are using more paper now than in the past. Environmentally concerned organizations are uneasy about the waste of paper. Some companies reuse unwanted documents by printing on the reverse side for internal reports. Many offices recycle used paper. Even if all paper were recycled once, however, it would have little impact in light of the historical increases in paper usage. Quieting the conscience of the over-consumer may even result in an overall net increase in consumption and waste. How have computers and low-cost printers contributed to the waste of paper? What could be done to decrease the amount of paperwork?

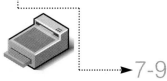

Investigating the World

1. Several questions should be considered before you purchase a printer:

   - What type of output (text, graphics, professional correspondence, etc.) will you produce?

   - Who will use, or receive, the output?

   - How much output will you need to produce?

   - Are multiple copies required?

   - Is color essential?

   - Are different fonts necessary?

   - Where will the printer be used?

   - Is the sound or speed of the printer a factor?

   - Is cost an issue?

   Answer each of these questions according to your current needs. Then, visit a computer store and find at least two printers that fit your requirements. Write the name of each printer and note its advantages and disadvantages. If you were going to purchase one of these printers, which would you buy? Why?

2. People are becoming increasingly concerned with ecological and health issues related to computer printers. Toner cartridges and printer ribbons, which must be changed periodically, are taking up space in the world's land-fills. It has been estimated that more than 12 million toner cartridges are disposed of each year. Workers in large offices complain about the noise pollution generated by several impact printers working at once and the possible effects on their hearing. Some office employees are anxious about the ozone emitted by poorly maintained laser printers. Ozone has been linked to respiratory problems, nausea, headaches, and possibly cancer. Using a library or other research facility, prepare a report on the ecological and health problems associated with printers and the steps that are being taken to address these problems.

Configuring Your Display

Summarizing the Lab

8

Instructions: Use the *Configuring Your Display* interactive lab to complete the following outline.

I. How does the computer create a display?

A computer's display system consists of the components illustrated in Figure 8.

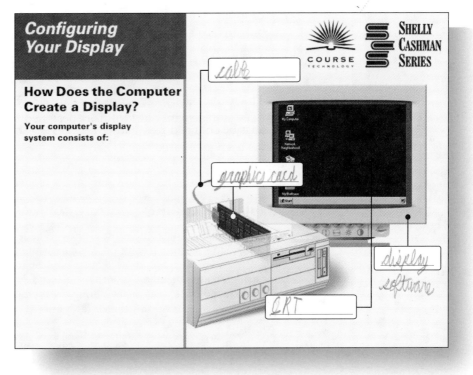

Figure 8

A monitor coupled with an input device, such as a keyboard, in a single unit is called a VDT (video display terminal). VDTs usually are connected to larger, multi-user computer systems.

II. The monitor

A computer's monitor is very similar to an ordinary _TV screen_ , but instead of tuning in broadcasts, it receives signals from the computer.

Personal computers typically use CRT, or cathode ray tube, technology. Technically, a CRT is the large tube inside a monitor. The front part of the tube is the display surface or screen.

Most portable computers use flat panel displays that employ either liquid crystal display (LCD) or gas plasma technologies. In an LCD display, a liquid crystal deposited between two sheets of polarizing metal is aligned by an electrical current. The liquid crystal prevents light from passing through and creates an image on the screen. This technology is used in digital watches, clocks, and calculators. Gas plasma screens substitute a neon gas for the liquid crystal material. Although gas plasma screens offer better resolution, they are more expensive and use more energy than LCD screens.

A. Computer monitors have _External knobs_ , or buttons, to adjust the picture.

B. The screen size of computer monitors is measured _diagonally_ , in inches, across the opposite corners of the screen.

The most widely used monitors are equivalent in size to a 17-inch television screen, but monitors designed for desktop publishing, graphics, or engineering applications come in larger sizes, such as 21 inches.

Exploring Online

Popular display manufacturers on the Web include Sony, NEC, ViewSonic, and MAG Innovision. In addition, Hercules Computer Technology hosts the World Wide Web Monitor Database, which includes a listing of monitor manufacturers and models with screen sizes. For more information on display technologies, visit the Exploring Computers Web page (www.scsite.com/expl.htm) and click Monitors.

C. The two main types of computer displays are *monochrome*
   and *R G B* .

   1. A *monochrome* monitor displays shades of a single color
      on black.

      Monochrome monitors are less expensive than color monitors
      and often are used by businesses for word processing, order entry,
      and other applications that do not require color. Using gray-
      scaling, which converts an image into pixels that are shades of
      gray, some monochrome monitors can display good quality
      graphic images.

   2. An *R G B* monitor displays images in full color.

      Color monitors are widely used with all types of computers
      because color monitor prices have fallen and most of today's
      software is written to display information in color.

      RGB monitors combine *Red* , *Green* ,
      and *Blue* color beams inside the video tube to
      reproduce the entire range of visible colors.

      In the simplest combinations, eight colors can be generated by
      combining the color beams: black (no color), red only, green only,
      blue only, magenta (red and blue), yellow (red and green), blue-
      green (blue and green), and white (red, green, and blue). As the
      intensity of the beams varies, many more hues can be generated.

D. A mask perforated with holes breaks the light beams into small dots
   on the computer screen. The distance between the dots, or
   dot pitch , determines how much detail the monitor
   can display.

   The perforated mask is called a shadow mask. The light beams move
   across and down the screen. Interlaced monitors illuminate every
   other line, then return to the top to illuminate the lines skipped.
   Noninterlaced monitors illuminate the entire screen more quickly in
   a single pass. The speed at which the entire screen is redrawn is
   called the refresh rate. If the refresh rate is too slow, images on the
   screen may oscillate or flicker.

III. What is a graphics display?

The computer's display is made up of tiny squares called picture
elements, or *pixels* .

The number of pixels actually displayed is determined by a combination
of the software in the computer, the capability of the video adapter
board, and the monitor itself.

A. The number of pixels on the screen determines the screen's _resolution_ . A display's resolution is measured in the number of pixels _across_ the screen times the number of pixels _down_ the screen. A typical resolution for a computer display is 640 pixels across by 480 down.

Monitor resolution is important, particularly when the monitor is used to display graphics or other nontext information. Due to separate development, printer resolution is expressed in dots per inch while monitor resolution is expressed in pixels per inch, which is dependent on dot pitch.

B. The number of colors that can be displayed on the screen at one time is called the _color depth_ . The range of available colors also is called the _pallet_ .

1. In a _standard 8-bit_ graphics system, 256 colors can be displayed on the screen.

2. In higher bit graphics displays, more bits are used to determine each pixel's color. Typical bit depths are _8 bit_ (256 colors), _16 bit_ (65,536 colors), and _32 bit_ (1.6 million colors). 24-bit and 32-bit images also are called _true color_ images.

Most PC color monitors display at least 256 colors at one time.

Monitors with _multisync_ capability can self-adjust to the display signals of many different computer systems.

Multisync, also called multiscanning, monitors are designed to work within a range of frequencies.

Exploring Your Computer

How large is the monitor on which you are working (remember, monitor size is measured diagonally across the screen)? How many colors does your monitor display? What is your monitor's resolution? What brand is your monitor?

IV. What is a graphics card?

The _graphics card_ is an expansion card that is installed in one of the slots of the PC. It converts pixel information into _video signals_ for display on the monitor. The card is equipped with its own memory, called _Video Random Access_ (VRAM), to store the pixel information. _Memory_

A. VGA, which stands for _Video Graphics Array_ ____, was the first PC graphics card to display 256 colors. A standard VGA resolution is ___640 x 480___ with ___65,536 colors___, which is used often for running Windows 95.

B. _Super VGA_ ____, or SVGA, improves on VGA by allowing an increase in colors and resolution. Typical SVGA resolutions are ___800 x 600___ and ___1024 x 768___ with thousands or even millions of colors.

Other video graphics standards include: CGA, or color graphics adapter, (640 x 200 with four displayed colors — one of the first cards to display color images), Hercules (720 x 348 with no color), and EGA or enhanced graphics adapter (640 x 480 with sixteen displayed colors). A concept called backward compatiblity allows graphics cards capable of higher resolution to run programs requiring lower resolution.

C. When more colors are displayed or resolution is increased, more ___memory (VRAM)___ is required to store the pixel information. The amount of memory on the graphics card determines the maximum combination of resolution and color depth.

$$\frac{4\ bits}{8\ bits} \times \frac{1448}{2848} \times \frac{1448}{2848} = VRAM\ (1\ mb)$$
$$= VRAM\ (4\ mb)$$
(resolution)

D. Some computer systems have a high-speed bus dedicated to graphics, called a ___VLB___. This bus bypasses the standard bus and communicates directly with the CPU, updating the screen at a much higher speed.

V. System configuration

Once the graphics card is installed, an application can be run from the Windows 95 _display's control panel_ to configure the system based on the new hardware. You then can modify the display's resolution and color palette using the _display's drivers setting_ tab in the Display Properties dialog box.

Exploring Windows 95

In addition to configuring the resolution and number of colors displayed by your monitor, you can use the Control Panel window to change your display's appearance and your monitor's energy saving features. Right-clicking the Windows 95 desktop, clicking Properties, then clicking the Appearance, Background, or Screen Saver tabs in the Display Properties dialog box allows you to change these options.

Evaluating the Results

True/False

Instructions: Circle **T** if the statement is true or **F** if the statement is false.

T F 1. The computer's display system consists of a video display, monitor cable, graphics card, and display driver software.

T F 2. A display's resolution is measured by the number of pixels across the screen times the number of pixels down the screen.

T **F** 3. Screen images drawn from a smaller palette have more gradual tones.

T **F** 4. When more colors are displayed or resolution is increased, less memory is required to store the pixel information.

T F 5. Resolution can be increased by sacrificing color depth, and vice versa.

Matching

Instructions: Write the letter of a description from the column on the right in front of each term in the column on the left.

_a_ 1. Monichrome

_e_ 2. RGB

_d_ 3. Resolution

_g_ 4. Color depth

_f_ 5. Graphics card

a. describes a monitor that displays images in shades of a single color on black

b. is a high-speed local bus dedicated to graphics

c. is a mask perforated with holes that break up the light beams as they pass through

d. is determined by the number of pixels on the screen

e. is a type of monitor that displays images in full color

f. converts pixel information into video signals for display on the monitor

g. is the number of colors that can be displayed on the screen at one time

Multiple Choice

Instructions: Circle the correct response.

1. What can be adjusted using the external controls on a computer monitor?
   a. resolution and color depth
   b. bus type and VRAM
   c. contrast and brightness
   d. all of the above

2. How is screen size measured?
   a. diagonally, in inches, across opposite corners of the screen
   b. down, in inches, from the top left corner to the bottom right corner
   c. across, in inches, from the top left corner to the top right corner
   d. as total screen area, in square inches

3. Which is *not* one of the three color beams used to reproduce the entire range of visible colors in a color monitor?
   a. red
   b. yellow
   c. blue
   d. green

4. What is dot pitch?
   a. the amount of memory on the graphics card
   b. the distance between pixels on the monitor screen
   c. the time required for the monitor to communicate with the CPU
   d. the number of bits used to determine each pixel's color

5. What was the first PC graphics card to display 256 colors at one time?
   a. CGA
   b. EGA
   c. VGA
   d. SVGA

Fill in the Blanks

Instructions: Place the correct word(s) in the blank in each sentence.

1. Monitors with _multisync_ capability can self-adjust to the display signals of many different computer systems.

2. The computer's display is made up of tiny squares called _pixels_.

3. _24 bit & 32 bit_ images are also called *true color* because their smooth range of color allows photorealistic images.

4. Some computer systems have a high-speed bus dedicated to graphics, called a(n) _VLB_, which bypasses the standard bus and communicates directly with the CPU.

5. You can change display resolution, color depth, and more through the Windows 95 _display properties_ dialog box.

Examining the Issues

1. The demand for larger computer displays continues to grow — even as the monitors themselves become thinner. Business users are seeing the benefits of larger screens which allow you to see more open windows at once and have a better view of documents and large spreadsheets. Users also are turning to thinner LCD monitors, which require only a quarter of the desk space of a comparable CRT and which do not create distortion. Lower heat emission, combined with power savings of up to 40 percent over comparable CRTs, appeal to just about everybody. At what point do you think the increase in display size and decrease in monitor width will stop? What will monitors be like ten years from now? Will employers use larger screens as a way to demand more productivity from workers?

2. Today, nearly all personal computers use a monitor. Although monitors are usually sold separately, it is hard to imagine buying a personal computer without one. Personal computers have even been sold with the monitor and system unit together in a single case, like the Apple Macintosh computer introduced in 1984. Will monitors still be the most popular computer display device twenty-five years from now? Why or why not? How might monitors be different?

Investigating the World

1. Visit a computer vendor and obtain information about the highest and lowest priced monitors. Record the names of the monitors, their costs, and the features available with each. Do you think the more expensive monitor is worth the difference in price? Why or why not? Examine a portable computer that uses a flat panel display. What type of screen is it (LCD or gas plasma)? How does the image compare with the most expensive CRT monitor? How does it compare with the least expensive CRT monitor?

2. Questions have been raised about health issues related to computer monitors. Although some believe that prolonged work at a monitor is less hazardous than a sunny day at the beach, others feel continued exposure to electromagnetic emissions from monitors can cause pregnancy problems or cancer. Certain European countries have published guidelines placing limits on monitor emissions. In America, many organizations have developed conservative policies, limiting the number of hours pregnant women work with a display screen or closely monitoring electromagnetic emissions. Using current periodicals or online services, research some of the health issues connected with computer monitors. Are the concerns justified? What is being done to address them? What steps, if any, should personal computer users take to protect themselves?

Maintaining Your Hard Drive

Summarizing the Lab

9

Instructions: Use the *Maintaining Your Hard Drive* interactive lab to complete the following outline.

I. What is a hard disk?

A hard disk is a hardware device that can store a large number of _programs/data_ in the form of files.

A hard disk is called secondary storage, or auxiliary storage, because it stores programs and data when they are not being processed. Memory, or RAM, is called primary storage because it temporarily stores programs and data that are being processed. Primary storage is fast, short term, and volatile. Secondary storage is slower, long term, and nonvolatile. Other forms of secondary storage include floppy disks, optical disks (CD-ROMs), magnetic tape, solid-state storage devices, and mass storage.

Exploring Windows 95

Microsoft Plus! is a Windows 95 software program that includes various tools for maintaining a hard drive. Among these are ScanDisk, which checks for and fixes errors on the hard disk; DriveSpace, which compresses the hard disk to free more space; and Disk Defragmenter, which reorganizes the files stored on the hard disk so they can be accessed more efficiently.

II. How a hard disk works

Most hard disks contain between one and four _platters_ coated with an oxide material that are mounted on a rotating spindle.

Personal computer hard disk drives typically are identified with the letter C, while the letters A, B, and D identify floppy disk and CD-ROM drives. Hard disks often are fixed, or permanently installed, in the computer system (although some portable computers have removable hard disk drives called disk cartridges). Floppy disks are a portable storage medium. Hard disk platters usually are aluminum, but some newer disks use glass or ceramic materials. Floppy disks (also called diskettes or floppies) consist of a circular piece of flexible mylar plastic coated with an oxide material and housed in a protective jacket. Both hard disks and floppy disks are examples of magnetic storage media, the most widely used type of storage.

Each surface of a hard disk's platter can be used to store data. _Read/Write_ heads attached to access arms swing out over the top and bottom surfaces of each platter.

The clearance between the heads and the disk surface is about ten millionths of an inch. If some form of contamination gets on the surface of the disk or if the read/write heads are jarred out of alignment, the heads can collide with and damage the disk surface and cause a loss of data. This event, known as a head crash, can be extremely costly in terms of both time and money.

A. _Access time_ is the short delay that results when the read/write heads move to where the beginning of the data is located.

Magnetic disks are referred to as direct-access storage devices because the computer can go immediately to the location where the desired data is stored. Magnetic tape, on the other hand, is considered a sequential storage medium because the computer must read each record in order on the tape until it locates the desired record.

The access time for a disk drive consists of two factors: _seek time_ and _rotational delay_.

1. _Seek time_ is the time it takes the read/write head to move across the width of the disk. Average seek time is considered the time it takes to move about halfway across the disk's width.

   Seek time is the largest part of total access time.

2. _Rotational delay_ is the delay while the platter rotates so the first item of data moves under the heads. The time it takes for half a rotation to occur is considered the average rotational delay.

Access time for a hard disk is between ten and twenty milliseconds (thousandths of a second), while access time for a floppy disk varies from about 150 milliseconds to 300 milliseconds. Hard disk access time is significantly less for two reasons: (1) a hard disk spins ten to twenty times faster than a floppy disk; and (2) a hard disk is always spinning, but a floppy disk spins only when a read or write command is received.

B. The read/write heads read data from the disk by picking up _electrical signals_ that are generated by the magnetic particles

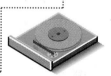

on the coated platters. The signals are converted into
digital form and loaded into the computer's memory unit.

C. When writing data to the disk, data from the computer's memory
unit is converted into _electrical signal_, which are stored as
positive and negative _charges_ on the platter.

Exploring Online

A number of hard drive manufacturers exist on the Web, including Seagate
and Western Digital.

If a problem is experienced with the hard drive, the DriveSavers Data
Recovery home page gives advice and assistance in recovering lost data. To
learn more about maintaining your hard drive, visit the Exploring
Computers Web page (www.scsite.com/expl.htm) and click Hard Drive.

D. _Data transfer rate_ is the time it takes to move a
given amount of data to or from the disk. Disk transfer rate is measured in _megabytes per second_ (million characters) of data
transferred per second.

Some computers use a disk cache to improve the apparent speed at
which data is transferred to and from a disk. Disk cache is an area of
memory set aside for the data most often read from the disk. When
data is requested, disk cache software looks first in the disk cache. If
the data is there, the slower disk read operation is avoided. A disk
cache program is included with both Windows and DOS operating
systems.

Access arms, with their attached read/write heads, move in fixed
patterns that cause the data to be written to both sides of the disk
in concentric circles called _tracks_. Each track is divided
further into a number of equal parts called _sectors_.

Tracks, cylinders, and sectors are defined on the disk surface when
the disk is formatted. The formatting process also erases any data
on the disk, analyzes the surface for defective spots, and establishes
a directory to record information about stored files. Hard disks and
floppy disks must be formatted before they can be used for secondary
storage.

Two methods can be used to write data to the disk:

1. In the _sector method_, the data is written to the disk
   track-by-track across a single surface, and then continued on the
   next surface.

Each sector contains a specified number of bytes; with PCs, for example, each sector holds 512 bytes. When data is requested from a disk using the sector method, the surface, track, and sector where the data is stored are indicated.

2. In the _cylinder method_, all tracks of the same number on each surface create a cylinder. Data is written to the same track on each of the surfaces before the read/write heads move on to the next track.

When data is accessed from a disk using the cylinder method, the cylinder, recording surface, and record number are specified.

III. How a hard disk stores files

Storage capacity is a function of the number of tracks per inch (tpi) and the number of bits that can be stored per inch of track (bpi).

Hard disk storage is measured in _megabytes or gigabytes_ each of which is equal to over _500,000 data_ typewritten pages of information. Most computer systems have hard disks that can store up to _500_ megabytes of data; newer systems have hard disks that can store 1, 2, or even 4 _or more gigabytes_ of data.

Floppy disks store considerably less data than hard disks. High-density (HD) floppy disks can store 1.44 megabytes on a 3½-inch disk.

Data compression software, such as PKZIP and WinZip, can be used to store more data on a disk. Data compression reduces storage requirements by substituting codes for repeated patterns of data. The substituted codes are filed in a table, which is used to restore the compressed data to its original form.

When a file is stored on the hard disk, it is split into small, equal parts; each part is stored in one of the _sectors_ on the hard disk. The space in which the file data is stored may not be _contiguous_; that is, it may not run across consecutive sectors.

IV. Fragmentation of the hard disk

If there are too few consecutive blank sectors to store a file, the hard disk skips to the next empty area and continues writing the file. When this happens repeatedly, the disk becomes _fragmented_. This increases the time it takes the computer to read the file because each portion of the file must be accessed individually.

In sequential access storage devices, such as magnetic tape, fragmentation is not a problem because data is stored serially.

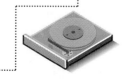

Exploring Your Computer

How much total storage space is on the hard drive in your computer? How much of the disk space is free and available? When was the last time your hard disk was defragmented? Has the hard disk been compressed by a disk compression program such as Stacker, Doublespace, or DriveSpace?

V. Maintaining an efficient hard disk

A. *Defragmentation* is accomplished by reading each file into memory and then writing it to a contiguous area of the hard disk.

Operating systems such as DOS 6.0 and Windows 95 include a defragmentation utility.

B. *Optimization* reduces the access time for the most frequently used files by moving them to the front of the hard disk.

The processes used to maintain the hard drive are illustrated in Figure 9.

To prevent the loss of data, it also is important to back up, or create another copy of, important programs and data on the hard disk. Floppy disks and magnetic tape are commonly used to back up at least some of the data stored on the hard disk of a personal computer.

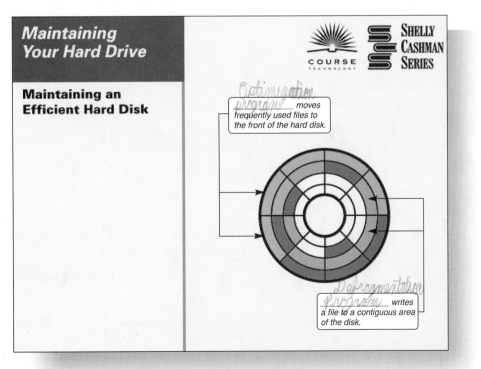

Maintaining Your Hard Drive

Maintaining an Efficient Hard Disk

COURSE TECHNOLOGY

SHELLY CASHMAN SERIES

Optimization program moves frequently used files to the front of the hard disk.

Defragmentation program writes a file to a contiguous area of the disk.

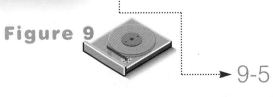

Figure 9

Evaluating the Results

True/False

Instructions: Circle **T** if the statement is true or **F** if the statement is false.

T F 1. The access time for a disk drive consists of two factors: seek time and rotational delay.

T **F** 2. The time it takes for a full rotation of the hard disk to occur is considered the average rotational delay.

T F 3. Newer hard disks can sustain a transfer rate of one to two megabytes per second.

T **F** 4. The cylinder method of writing data to the disk increases the amount of movement, which decreases the speed.

T F 5. When a file is stored on the hard disk, the file is split into small equal parts, which are each stored in one of the sectors on the hard disk.

Matching

Instructions: Write the letter of a description from the column on the right in front of each term in the column on the left.

_c_ 1. Platters

_d_ 2. Access arms

_a_ 3. Tracks

_g_ 4. Sectors

_e_ 5. Cylinders

a. narrow recording bands forming concentric circles around a hard disk surface

b. spindles on which disk surfaces rotate in the hard disk drive

c. rigid disks coated on either side with an oxide material that stores data as magnetic charges

d. mechanisms that swing out over the top and bottom surfaces of each hard disk

e. all concentric circles of the same number on each hard disk surface

f. two or more complete hard disk surfaces used to store the operating system

g. equal parts into which the concentric circles around a hard disk surface are divided

Multiple Choice

Instructions: Circle the correct response.

1. How many platters are mounted on a rotating spindle in most personal computer hard disk drives?
   a. one or two
   b. between one and four
   c. between eight and sixteen
   d. between fifty and one hundred

2. What is seek time?
   a. the time it takes to locate a file in memory and write it to the disk
   b. the time it takes for the platter to rotate so the first data item is under the read/write heads
   c. the time it takes to transfer data from the disk into memory
   d. the time it takes the read/write head to move across the width of the disk

3. In what method of writing data to the disk is data written track-by-track across a single surface, then continued down to the next surface?
   a. sector method
   b. cylinder method
   c. cluster method
   d. file method

4. Hard disk storage is measured in what units?
   a. kilobytes and centibytes
   b. megabytes and gigabytes
   c. millibytes and kilobytes
   d. dekabytes and megabytes

5. What procedure reduces access time for the most frequently used files by moving them to the front of the hard disk?
   a. defragmentation
   b. polarization
   c. optimization
   d. segmentation

Fill in the Blanks

Instructions: Place the correct word(s) in the blank in each sentence.

1. A(n) _hard drive_ is a hardware device that can store a large number of programs and data in the form of files.

2. _Read/Write head_ attached to access arms swing out over the top and bottom surfaces of each hard disk platter, generating electronic impulses.

3. The short delay that results as the read/write heads move to the beginning of where the data is located on a hard disk is known as _seek time_.

4. The time it takes to move a given amount of data to or from the disk is known as _data transfer rate_.

5. A(n) _fragmented_ disk increases the time the computer takes to read files because each portion of the file must be accessed separately from noncontiguous sectors.

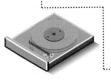

Examining the Issues

1. When a file is deleted from a hard disk, it is not physically erased or removed from the disk. Instead, the computer's operating system simply makes the sectors where the file was contained available for new data. Until another file is written to these sectors, the *deleted* file remains stored on the disk. What are the advantages of this system? What are the disadvantages?

2. It is estimated that data loss costs American companies approximately $4 billion each year. Data stored on hard disks can disappear as a result of natural disasters, computer viruses, or head crashes. Despite the risk, a study has shown that less than 35 percent of all companies have backup policies stipulating regular procedures for making copies of stored information. Why do so few companies back up their data? If you were the CEO of a large company, what backup policy would you establish? What would you do to see that it was enforced?

Investigating the World

1. Many companies store large amounts of information on hard disks that are permanently mounted inside the computer. As a result, the problem of data security has become an important issue. No company can afford to have sensitive information on customers or product development stolen by industrial spies or dissatisfied employees. Visit a large firm and interview an employee on data security. How are records protected? Who has access to sensitive data? Have there ever been problems with data security? If so, what measures have been taken to make sure the problems do not recur?

2. Visit a computer store and obtain information on the different types of hard disk drives available for personal computers. Summarize your findings and include data on price, storage capacity, and access speed. Calculate the cost per megabyte of storage for each disk drive. If you were purchasing a hard disk drive for your own personal computer, which would be best for your current needs? Why? Do you think the same disk drive would be adequate five years from now? Why or why not?

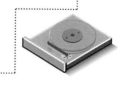

Exploring the Computers of the Future

Summarizing the Lab

Instructions: Use the *Exploring the Computers of the Future* interactive lab to complete the following outline.

I. Computers of the future

Innovation in the computer industry has focused on developing computers that provide increased functionality and fit more naturally into people's lives and activities.

A. _New production techniques_ and _better quality materials_ are reducing the size of microprocessor chip components, leading to smaller computers with more processing capability and microcomputers embedded in objects and technological devices.

Early general-purpose computers such as the Mark I and ENIAC were room-sized, performed only a few calculations each second, and consumed so much electricity that when they were turned on city lights dimmed. The microprocessor chips in today's PCs are pocket-watch-sized, perform millions of instructions per second, and consume about as much electricity as a television set.

Smart cards are credit-card-sized pieces of plastic with embedded microprocessor chips that can store and process information and transactions.

The U.S. Marine Corps currently issues smart cards to recruits who use them instead of cash. Smart cards also can be used for employee time and attendance tracking and security applications. People may someday carry smart cards containing their complete medical histories, providing up-to-date medical records.

B. _Voice input capability_ gives computers the capability to store and forward messages for their users, and to make voice annotations to documents.

Because people can speak much faster than they can type (about 200 words per minute compared to about 40 words per minute), some experts believe voice input eventually will be the most common way to operate a computer. Voice input is especially welcomed by people with certain disabilities.

C. _Voice recognition_ software enables a computer to recognize spoken commands by processing the physical sound waves and using pattern matching to recognize the words being said.

Some voice recognition systems are speaker dependent, which means that the computer must be trained to identify an individual user's voice. Larger voice recognition systems use voice templates — multiple word patterns with male and female voices, as well as regional accents. These systems are speaker independent, because most users will not have to train the system to their individual speech patterns.

D. _Agents_ are software modules that exist within an application or environment to facilitate work by operating intelligently with users.

The agents in Microsoft's productivity software, called *wizards*, can be used for such diverse tasks as creating reports or brochures, drawing charts, developing presentations, and sending out party invitations. Network agents generally are considered more intelligent than wizards because they perform their work on remote computers without user prompts, and then bring the results back to the user.

E. _Virtual Reality_ systems *immerse* a person in a simulated environment by surrounding the user with sight and sound.

Virtual reality (VR) software already is being employed by architects to let clients experience proposed construction or remodeling changes. VR has been used by scientists at NASA, surgeons, engineers, urban planners, and the U.S. Army. VR also is being used on the Internet for games, chat rooms, and more. Although still in its early stages, the increasing power of computers and the potential applications of VR have kept millions of dollars flowing into research.

F. _Cross Platform_, a _software_ allows the same application to work on a variety of computers, so that a document created using Java can be run on Windows 95 or a UNIX machine.

The differences among operating systems have made the development of cross-platform software a daunting task.

G. For years, most of the telephone network was connected by copper cable. Today, _fiber optic cable_, a kind of wire made of glass, can transmit an almost unlimited amount of digital information.

With fiber-optic cable, data is converted into light pulses and transmitted by laser. Fiber-optic cable is more difficult to install and modify than metal wiring. Nevertheless, fiber-optic cable offers several advantages over copper cable: higher volume, greater speed (about 10,000 times faster), lower error rate, increased security, and longer life. Japan plans to connect every home and business to fiber-optic cable by the year 2010.

Integrated services Digital Network (ISDN) can be used to convert sections of existing copper cable — say, from your home to the local exchange — to digital transmission. This speeds up the transfer of data dramatically and makes applications such as radio broadcasts on the Internet possible.

H. _Wireless Computers_ use radio frequency (RF) or infrared (IR) technology to communicate without a physical connection, enabling computers to communicate from multiple locations.

RF uses radio waves to communicate with a local antenna assigned to a specific geographic area called a _cell_. Individual cells are one to ten miles in width and use between 50 and 75 radio channels. The cell antenna relays a signal to a mobile telephone switching office, where it can enter the regular phone system. Personal digital assistants (PDAs), the small hand-held computing devices used by mobile workers, usually have a wireless capability to send and receive data.

II. The office of the future

Computers can increase worker productivity by supporting collaboration, communication, and the ability to access and use information effectively.

A. _Simulations_ will be significantly improved by computers. _virtual reality_ will be used for training in high risk professions, while _Computer Aided Design_ technologies will let people experience and evaluate new products before production.

Computer-aided design (CAD) technology uses a computer and special graphics software to assist in product planning. CAD eliminates laborious drafting and allows designers to dynamically change a product and then view the results of those changes. A related technology, called computer-aided engineering (CAE), uses computers to test product designs by simulating the effects of such factors as wind, temperature, weight, and stress on computer prototypes.

B. _Today, almost every office_ use electronic devices to help people work with and share information more effectively. Today, client server networks and e-mail are keeping coworkers connected. This trend will continue as technologies such as Internet telephones and video conferencing become increasingly common.

Many companies also are posting Web pages on internal networks called _Internets_ . Employees use a Web browser to view pages on meetings, corporate polices, financial updates and more, just as they would view pages on the Web.

Exploring Windows 95

What does the future hold for Windows 95? According to Microsoft, prospective releases will incorporate some of the capabilities currently offered in Microsoft's other operating system, Windows NT. Many of the features of Windows 95, such as the graphical user interface and Plug-and-Play, also will be included in future versions of Windows NT, allowing new software applications to run on both platforms.

C. _Information_ is increasingly being created, used, and maintained in electronic form. Technologies such as _scanning_ and _OCR_ allow information to be converted from paper documents to electronic form and vice versa. _Document exchange_ allow information to be converted from one format to another.

Digital convergence describes the merging of technologies and products from the communications, entertainment, publishing, and computing industries. This merger is made possible by the conversion of information from these industries into a digital form that can be processed, stored, and distributed by computers. Several major newspapers and magazines already offer online versions of their publications. An advantage of electronic documents is that they can incorporate both video and sound data elements.

III. The home of the future

Technology is used in the home to save time and help people pursue their interests. Three types of future technologies for the home are illustrated in Figure 10 on the next page.

A. _Telecommuting_ is the ability of individuals to use new technologies to work from home. People can attend meetings and communicate face to face while they are at home through _Personal Computing_ and teleconferencing.

Telecommuting provides flexibility, allowing companies and employees to increase productivity and, at the same time, meet the needs of individual employees. Advantages of telecommuting include: reduced commute time, elimination of the need to travel in poor weather conditions, a convenient and comfortable work environ- ment for disabled employees, and the ability to combine work and family responsibilities. Some cities have upgraded local communications channels to attract telecommuters.

B. _Integrated control of a variety of devices_, including security, environment, lighting, and sprinkler systems, will be provided by computers of the future.

Most existing home control systems were installed after the home was built and often consist of separate systems to control each set of devices. Chips are being designed, however, that will allow all appliances, lighting systems, and other home products to be net-worked together and controlled by a single system using a consistent set of commands. Bill Gates, CEO of Microsoft, has 100 microcomputers built into his _smart home_. Residents and visitors wear pins that identify them and allow the house to adapt to their tastes —adjusting room temperatures, displaying favorite art images, playing personal music preferences, and gradually turning lights on and off as people enter and leave rooms.

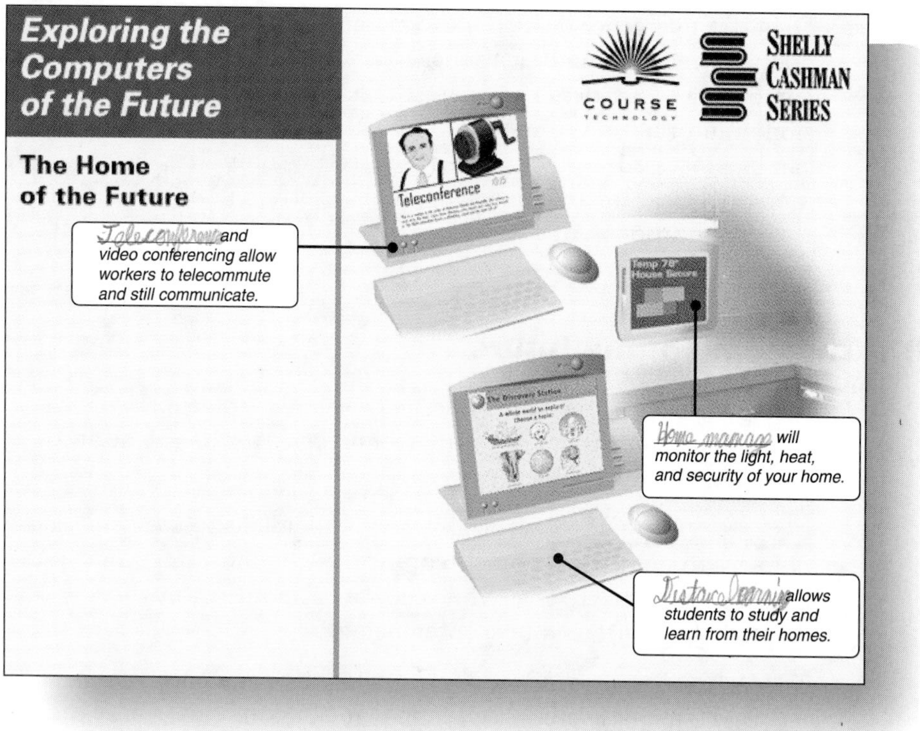

**Exploring the
Computers
of the Future**

COURSE TECHNOLOGY

SHELLY CASHMAN SERIES

**The Home
of the Future**

Teleconference and video conferencing allow workers to telecommute and still communicate.

Teleconference

Temp 72° House Secure

The Discovery Series

Home manage will monitor the light, heat, and security of your home.

Distance learning allows students to study and learn from their homes.

Figure 10

C. _Computer Aided Instructions (CAI)_ is a rapidly growing area in education. PCs will enable students to take advantage of _distance learning_ in their homes.

CAI software can be classified into three types: drill and practice (which uses a flash-card approach to learning), tutorial (which uses text, graphics, and sound to teach concepts), and simulation (which teaches by creating models of real-life situations). Trade schools, colleges, and universities now are offering distance learning classes, transmitting lessons and assignments between the student and the school over communications lines like the Internet.

D. _Video games_ are one way home computers are used for entertainment today. More powerful computers can create exciting, interactive game experiences with the illusion of reality. Computers also may entertain by connecting to other media and supporting creativity.

Popular types of entertainment software include arcade games, board games, simulations, and interactive graphics programs. Some games can be played in groups using a network, allowing players to adjust the level of play to match their abilities. Computers also are used by hobbyists to design quilt and stained glass patterns, run model trains, organize collections, and compose and play musical scores. Internet TVs (or WebTVs) even let you channel-surf through Web pages.

E. <u>Home management</u>, including organizing schedules, managing finances, and even providing assistance in home improvement and repair, will be performed more efficiently in the future with the help of computers.

PC software is available to assist with balancing checkbooks, making household budgets, and preparing tax returns. In addition, using personal computers to transmit and receive data over telephone lines allows people to pay bills and perform other financial transactions, and provides access to a wealth of information and services from online service providers.

Exploring Your Computer

Consider some of the future advances in technology discussed in this lab. Which do you think will have the greatest effect on the way you live and work? Why? Which has the most appeal to you? Why? How do you think this technology might be implemented in your computer?

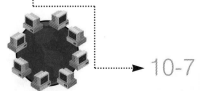

Evaluating the Results

True/False

Instructions: Circle **T** if the statement is true or **F** if the statement is false.

T (**F**) 1. New production techniques and better quality materials are continually increasing the size of the components inside microprocessor chips. *reducing*

(**T**) **F** 2. Virtual reality systems often use special accessories, such as goggles or gloves, to make the virtual environment seem real and allow the user to take actions within it.

T (**F**) 3. Most portable computers require a wireless connection to communicate.

(**T**) **F** 4. In the future, the trend toward interconnected work environments will continue, with technologies such as client-server networks, e-mail, Internet phones, and video conferencing becoming increasingly common.

(**T**) **F** 5. In the office of the future, the form in which information is stored and used will be determined primarily by computers.

Matching

Instructions: Write the letter of a description from the column on the right in front of each term in the column on the left.

_e_ 1. Voice input

_a_ 2. Handwriting recognition

_d_ 3. Agents

_f_ 4. Virtual reality

_g_ 5. Cross-platform software

a. software that can be taught to recognize an individual's unique style of writing

b. software that uses computers to control production equipment

c. software that deals with values that are not precise and have a degree of uncertainty

d. software modules that exist within an application to facilitate work

e. software that allows users to enter data and issue commands with spoken words

f. software that creates an artificial environment that can be experienced by the computer user

g. software that will work with a variety of different computers and operating systems

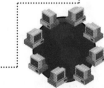

Multiple Choice

Instructions: Circle the correct response.

1. What two types of software use pattern matching to convert what a user
   has input into a form that the computer understands?
   a. voice input software and agent software
   b. agent software and voice recognition software
   c. voice recognition software and handwriting recognition software
   d. handwriting recognition software and virtual reality software

2. Which of the following is *not* an advantage that fiber-optic cables have over
   copper cables?
   a. larger capacity
   b. easier installation
   c. increased speed
   d. clearer signals

3. Like cellular phones, wireless computers use what technology to communicate without a physical connection?
   a. radio frequency (RF)
   b. microwave (MW)
   c. laser-beam (LB)
   d. infrared (IR)

4. What is computer-aided design (CAD)?
   a. technology that uses computers to control production equipment and
      scheduling
   b. technology that integrates the entire manufacturing process using
      computers
   c. technology that allows computer users to alter the motherboard and
      peripherals
   d. technology that lets people experience and evaluate products before
      production

5. In the home of the future, technologies such as fax machines, e-mail, and
   video conferencing will help people most in which of the following areas?
   a. telecommuting
   b. control of home systems
   c. entertainment
   d. home management

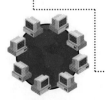

Fill in the Blanks

Instructions: Place the correct word(s) in the blank in each sentence.

1. A(n) _smart card_ is a credit-card-sized piece of plastic with an embedded microprocessor chip that can store and process information and transactions.

2. _Virtual Reality_ systems often use special accessories, such as goggles or gloves, to make the environment seem real and allow the user to take actions within it.

3. _Fiber Optic Cable_ are a new type of wire made of glass that can transmit an almost infinite amount of information.

4. _Scanning & OCR_ programs allow paper documents to be converted into electronic form, and vice versa.

5. _Teleconferencing_ allows people to attend meetings and communicate face to face while at separate locations.

Examining the **Issues**

1. As tuition costs rise, students increasingly are aware of the other financial burdens — books, supplies, room, board, and so on — associated with a college education. In the future, however, they may face an additional expense: mandatory computers. Already, one university requires that entering freshmen purchase a specific laptop computer at a cost of $3,000. Another university insists that every student have uninterrupted, 24-hour access to some kind of personal computer. Students at both schools have protested the new mandates, claiming the additional expense will make college unaffordable for some students and threaten the economic diversity of the student population. Are the computer policies of these schools justified? Why or why not? What impact would personal computer requirements have on the student body? Why?

2. One of the strongest high school memories for many people is dissecting a frog in biology class. In the future, however, virtual reality software may replace the scalpel and frog cadaver. Programs such as *Virtual Frog* and *MacInvertebrate* approximate real dissections as students use tweezers on the computer screen to place virtually dissected tissues in a petri dish. The experience may be enhanced with color-coded organs, cheers for correct identifications, and even movies of the digestive, reproductive, and skeletal systems. While the virtual reality software has won the praise of squeamish students and animal-rights activists, the National Association of Biology Teachers continues to favor real dissections for instruction. Should a virtual reality experience take the place of genuine dissections in high school classes? Why or why not?

Investigating the World

1. Visit a software vendor and do one of the following:

   - Try out a software application that includes an agent or wizard, such as Microsoft Word or Microsoft Excel. For what purpose is the wizard used? What are the advantages of using a wizard? What are the disadvantages? Is the final result produced by the wizard more or less attractive, creative, or distinctive than what you could have done on your own? Why? Would you be more likely to buy an application with or without a wizard? Why?

   - Find at least two different software applications that can be used to assist with similar home accounting tasks, such as balancing checkbooks, making household budgets, or preparing tax returns. What is the name of each application? What is the cost? What are the hardware requirements? If possible, test each one , performing the same tasks. Which one is easier to use? Why? Does either application offer more capabilities? What are they? On the basis of your examination, which software, if any, would you be most inclined to purchase? Why?

2. Volunteer to help out in a primary or secondary school class while it is using computer-aided instruction (CAI). What software is being used? What is it trying to teach? What type of software (drill and practice, tutorial, or simulation) is it? Could the same topic be taught more effectively using a different type of software? Why or why not? Could the topic be taught better by a teacher? Why? How do the students respond to CAI? From your observation, what are the advantages of CAI? What are the disadvantages? In general, are your feelings about computer-aided instruction positive or negative? Why?

Connecting to the Internet

Summarizing the Lab

11

Instructions: Use the *Connecting to the Internet* interactive lab to complete the following outline.

I. What is the Internet?

The Internet (also called the Net) is a _Vast network_ of computer networks that links people, educational institutions, and corporations worldwide.

A network uses communications channels to share data, information, hardware, and software among connected computers. The Internet is composed of INTERconnected NETworks. Begun in 1969 as a way for government computers to communicate with each other, the Internet expanded to include universities and private research sites. In the early 1990s, new software called Web browsers simplified access for people outside the scientific and academic communities. Today, the Internet has more than 40 million users located in 200 countries, 100,000 connected networks, and 12 million host computers or sites. Since 1988, the Internet has doubled in size — and it continues to grow explosively each year.

II. Communicating with the Internet

The most common Internet services available are: _Electronic Mail_, _File Transfer Protocol_, _Terminal Sessions_, _News_, _Internet Relay Chat_, _Gopher_, and _WWW_.

A. Using _Electronic Mail_, or _E-Mail_, is just like writing a letter. Text files are created, addressed, and sent to the recipient's e-mail address.

Electronic mail is the most widely used service on the Internet. When a message arrives, it is stored in a special file, called the mail box, on the destination computer using the recipient's account name as the file name. After issuing a command to read incoming mail, the recipient can save, delete, reply to, or otherwise manage the message.

The standard format for an e-mail address is:

<u>User name</u> @ <u>Domain</u> . <u>type</u>

1. <u>User name</u> is the person's account name.

   Usernames must be unique to the domain. They often consist of a first initial and last name. Because spaces are not allowed in usernames, underscores may be substituted (for example, john_smith@ibm.com).

2. <u>Domain</u> is the location where the user's account is set up.

   The domain can be more than one word, separated by periods or dots (for example, jsmith@finance.ibm.com). This might happen when the account is set up on a local area network (LAN) that is part of an organization with several different LANs.

3. <u>Type</u> is an abbreviation for the kind of organization where the account is located.

   There are a small number of top-level domain types. In addition to com (commercial organizations), edu (educational organizations), and org (other organizations), some other types are mil (US military groups), gov (US government institutions), int (international organizations) and net (network resources).

Informal rules, called e-mail etiquette or netiquette, have been developed for using e-mail. These rules include keeping messages short and distribution lists to a minimum, avoiding gossip, respecting the confidentiality of others, and not engaging in *flaming*, or sending rude, inflammatory messages.

Because e-mail messages are read without benefit of hearing the sender's tone of voice or seeing any facial expression, senders sometimes include symbols to convey their mood. To interpret these symbols, often called smileys, a reader rotates the page 90° clockwise. Common smileys include — **:)** (smile), **: (** (frown), **;)** (wink), **: I** (indifference), and **: D** (laugh out loud).

B. <u>FTP</u>, or <u>File Transfer Protocol</u>, is a way to send and receive files over the Internet.

Using FTP software, users can connect to certain computers on the Internet that act as <u>FTP Sites</u>. These computers are servers that send users the file they request.

Archie is special software that can be used to search for specific files. Archie returns the Internet address of the files located, and FTP then can be used to retrieve them.

Files on FTP sites often are compressed to save downloading time, in which case a program like PKZIP or WINZIP is needed to extract the compressed file.

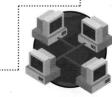

Exploring Online

Several search tools and directories are available to assist in navigating the Internet. Examples include Yahoo!, Lycos, Excite, Hotbot, and WebCrawler. You can access one of these World Wide Web sites and perform a search for a topic that interests you, such as a favorite sports team, music group, or TV program. For more details about using search tools on the Internet, visit the Exploring Computers Web page (www.scsite.com/expl.htm) and click Internet.

C. Using _telnet_ , distant computer systems having specialized programs can be accessed through the Internet.

Some remote computer sites have Telnet accounts that can be used to reach special resources, such as university library catalogs and the Library of Congress.

D. _News groups_ are message areas where people can discuss a common area of interest.

Newsgroups are available on almost any subject, including such diverse topics as vendor products, recipes, gardening, music, and more. A newsgroup name, such as rec.sport.golf, begins with a category name and is followed by one or more words that narrow down the main topic of the group. Category names include: comp (computer topics), talk (discussion), alt (alternative discussions), biz (business), info (information), misc (miscellaneous topics), rec (recreational topics), and sci (scientific topics).

Usenet is an informal group of systems that exchange news on a variety of topics. An article posted to a newsgroup on one system is duplicated throughout Usenet, with each participating computer site eventually receiving a copy.

E. _Internet Relay Chat_ , or IRC, also allows you to discuss topics of interest with others. Unlike newsgroups, however, IRC occurs in real-time, so you get immediate responses to your comments. IRC allows you to select a topic, called a _channel_ , and join in the discussion. IRC channels are available on almost any subject imaginable, but, if you do not find a channel you like, you can easily start your own.

F. _Gopher_ is a text viewer that can be used to follow linkages, called _hyperlinks_ , between different documents anywhere in the world. Text documents that contain hyperlinks are known as _hypertext_ .

A gopher server presents a hierarchy of menus through which the user pages until the desired file is located.

Veronica is a search tool used within a gopher that reduces the time required to hunt through gopher servers.

Text-based gopher hypertext menus are being replaced by hyper-media documents on the World Wide Web.

G. The _WWW_ is the entire collection of hyperlinked documents, called Web pages, containing images, sounds, and even video. This collection is stored in computer systems around the world called _Web sites_ . Web pages are viewed using a _Web Browser_ .

The World Wide Web combines e-mail, FTP, newsgroups, and gopher. Using hypertext links, related information is grouped together for easy retrieval. Clicking a link (also called an anchor) on a Web page leads to other text files, graphics, sounds, or video.

Web browsers have a graphical interface that can be used to look at multimedia documents on host computers around the world. *Surfing* is a slang term for browsing the Internet.

III. Gaining access to the Internet

Employees of a company connected to the Internet and students at most secondary schools are able to take advantage of the Internet. Home users can access the Internet by subscribing to a _service provider_

Exploring Windows 95

Windows 95 comes with software that links users to the The Microsoft Network (MSN), an online service offered by Microsoft that provides access to the Internet. Microsoft also offers software for connecting to the Internet and a World Wide Web browser in the Microsoft Plus! software package.

Fees for service providers vary greatly. Some have a higher fixed monthly charge with a low hourly connect-time fee. Others have a lower fixed monthly charge and a higher hourly connect-time fee.

During normal business hours, some public libraries and local governments offer limited public Internet access.

IV. Connecting to the Internet from home

Accessing an Internet service requires a _modem_ , which enables a computer to transfer information over a telephone line, and _dial-up software_ , which tells the modem to connect to the service, installed on a personal computer.

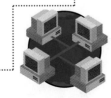

Exploring Your Computer

Is your computer connected to the Internet? If so, are you connected directly to the Internet through a network, or do you dial into it through a modem? What Internet services described in this lab are you able to use?

The word modem is a combination of the words *mo*dulate (to change a computer's digital signal into a sound or analog signal) and *dem*odulate (to convert an analog signal into a digital signal). Dialing software stores, selects, and dials telephone numbers of computers that can be called.

Two types of Internet connections are:

A. With _remote login_ service, the computer and modem are used to connect to another computer attached to the Internet. Mail, news, and other programs are then run on the _distant computer_ .

B. A _SLIP_ (Serial Line Internet Protocol) or _PPP_ (Point to Point Protocol) account enables a computer to communicate over telephone lines with a group of networked computers. With SLIP or PPP, all information is sent directly to _your computer_ .

V. Structure of the Internet

Devices that play a role in getting a message across the Internet include those illustrated in Figure 11 on the next page.

A. When a user sends a message, the message first is sent over telephone lines to the _local network_ that handles the user's account.

B. When the message arrives, the _network server_ determines where the message should go.

   The server is a computer dedicated to handling the communication needs of the other computers in the network.

C. If the message is to be sent to another network, the server sends it to a _router_ , which sends messages between networks using a variety of communications channels. These may include copper or fiber-optic telephone cables, microwave, or satellite transmissions.

   A router is an intelligent network-connecting device that can route communications directly to the appropriate network.

D. When the message reaches its destination network, a router passes it to the _network gateway_ . The message is transferred to the _network server_ , which stores it in the recipient's personal electronic mail box.

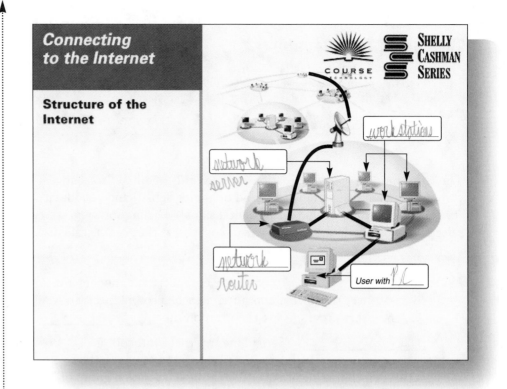

Figure 11

A gateway is a combination of hardware and software that allows users on one network to access the resources on a different network.

E. When the user connects to the network, the server transfers the message to his or her personal computer.

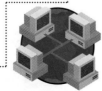

Evaluating the **Results**

True/False

Instructions: Circle **T** if the statement is true or **F** if the statement is false.

T F 1. The Internet is a vast network of computer networks that links millions of people and thousands of educational institutions and corporations world wide.

T **F** 2. Newsgroups are similar to traditional broadcast news in that people can read the contents of the group but cannot contribute to it.

T **F** 3. Hyperlinked documents that contain images, sound, and even video are known as Web sites.

T **F** 4. When your computer is connected to the Internet using a remote log-in service, all information from any e-mail or news programs run is sent directly to your computer.

T F 5. Devices that play a role when one user sends information to another across the Internet include network servers, network routers, computer workstations, and modems.

Matching

Instructions: Write the letter of a description from the column on the right in front of each term in the column on the left.

_g_ 1. FTP

_f_ 2. Telnet

_e_ 3. Newsgroups

_d_ 4. Gopher

_b_ 5. World Wide Web

a. a program used to display information about another's computer account

b. the entire collection of hyperlinked documents stored in computer systems around the world

c. a text viewer that can be used to follow linkages between different documents

d. a search tool that helps to locate and retrieve documents on the Internet

e. message areas where people can discuss a common area of interest

f. a protocol that allows users access to programs and data on a distant computer

g. a way to send and receive files over the Internet

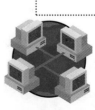

Multiple Choice

Instructions: Circle the correct response.

1. What is the standard format for an e-mail address?
   a. username.type@domain
   b. domain@type.username
   c. type.username@domain
   d. username@domain.type

2. What is the *com* extension short for in an e-mail address?
   a. community group
   b. commercial organization
   c. communications personnel
   d. communist party

3. To access an Internet service from home, what must be installed on your personal computer?
   a. a server and workstation
   b. a modem and dialing software
   c. a gateway and router
   d. gopher and hypertext

4. What type of Internet connection enables a distant computer to communicate with a group of networked computers in the same way they communicate with each other?
   a. remote log-in
   b. SLIP or PPP
   c. archie
   d. FTP

5. What is the function of a network server?
   a. it determines where a message coming into the network should go
   b. it sends messages between networks using a variety of communications channels
   c. it receives all incoming messages and stores them in a mailbox
   d. it converts digital signals into analog signals that can travel over telephone lines

Fill in the Blanks

Instructions: Place the correct word(s) in the blank in each sentence.

1. Using __e - Mail__ , a common Internet service, involves creating a text file, addressing the file, and sending it to the recipient's address.

2. Linkages between different documents, called __hyperlinks__ , may connect files anywhere in the world.

3. Web pages are viewed using a(n) __Web Browser__ .

4. Home computer users can access the Internet by subscribing to a(n) __Service Provider__ that offers connections to the Internet for a small monthly fee.

5. __Network Router__ send messages between networks using a variety of communications channels, such as telephone lines, microwaves, fiber-optic cable, and satellite transmissions.

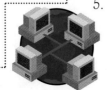

Examining the **Issues**

1. The Internet has had a major impact on the way people use computers. Now, some companies are expecting the Internet to have an impact on the computers themselves. Several innovative manufacturers offer an alternative to the current PC called the *NC*, or network computer. The NC provides only the most-used functions: access to the Internet, word processing, e-mail, and video conferencing. Any additional software required can be downloaded from the Internet. NCs require fewer components and are about as powerful as the early 486 PCs, with a flat-panel monochrome display, keyboard, mouse, and modem. The NC does not have a hard drive, but relies instead on networks to handle any storage needs. Best of all, the NC sells for $500 – $1000. Is the NC the computer of the future, eventually replacing the PC? Why or why not? What problems might an NC user have?

2. Certain groups have suggested that dangerous information, along with material that is discriminatory, inflammatory, confidential, or obscene, should not be available on the Internet. They propose that controls be placed over the content of newsgroups, files, and documents on the Internet. Others maintain, however, that any restrictions threaten free speech. In addition, because the Internet is global in scope and standards for acceptable material vary from country to country, state to state, and even community to community, controls are unrealistic. Should controls be placed over the material available on the Internet? Why or why not?

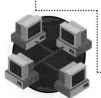

Investigating the World

1. Most home users access the Internet through a service provider. Some of the more popular service providers are: America Online (800-827-6364), Prodigy (800-776-3449), CompuServe (800-848-8199), The Microsoft Network (800-386-5550), Delphi (800-695-4005), Netcom (800-NETCOM1), AT&T WorldNet (800-WORLDNET), and MCI Internet (800-550-0927). Call at least three of these service providers. What types of services do they offer? How is access to the Internet provided? Is a particular type of computer, operating system, modem, or interface required? What are the membership fees? Are there any other fees (such as an hourly access fee, minimum monthly charge, or added cost for certain services)? From the information you receive, in which service provider would you be most interested? Why?

2. One piece of computer hardware that is essential to access the Internet is a modem. Visit a computer vendor and compare several modems. List the characteristics of each, including such items as the transmission rate, the manufacturer, the cost, and whether it is an internal or external modem. Consider the type of personal computer you already have, or would like to purchase, and how you would like to use the Internet. On the basis of the information you have gathered, which modem would you be most likely to purchase? Why?

The World Wide Web

12

Summarizing the Lab

Instructions: Use the *World Wide Web* interactive lab to complete the following outline.

I. What is the World Wide Web?

In 1991, a programmer developed a program that created documents, called _web pages_, with built-in links to other documents on the Internet. These links, called _hyperlinks_, can be used to move quickly from one document to the next, no matter where the documents are stored.

The collection of hyperlinked documents has become known as the _WWW or Web_.

II. How does the World Wide Web work?

The Internet locations where Web pages are stored are _web sites_. Multiple Web sites may exist on the same computer. Web sites are located on computers around the world that are connected to the _Internet_. To view pages at these Web sites, a computer first must connect to the Internet.

III. Web pages

Web pages may contain several types of files, including text, graphics, animation, video, and executable programs. There are two types of Web pages:

- _Hypertext_ link text documents to other text documents.
- _Hypermedia_ link text, video, graphics, and sound.

A. Web page links

A Web page can have three types of hyperlinks:

- _Target_ move from one location in a document to another location within the same document.

- _Relative_ move from one document to another document on the same computer.

- _Absolute_ move to another document on a different computer.

Hyperlinks to other documents are displayed either as underlined text of a different color or as a graphic. When the mouse pointer is positioned over a hyperlink, the mouse pointer changes to a small hand with a pointing finger.

Hyperlinks make it possible to learn about subjects in a nonlinear manner. Reading a book from cover to cover — learning a subject in a straight line from beginning to end — is learning in a linear manner. Branching off and investigating related topics as they are encountered is a nonlinear way of learning. The ability to branch from one related topic to another makes hyperlinks a powerful tool and the Internet an interesting place to explore.

Jumping from one Web page to another is called _web surfing_ .

B. Creating a Web page

Web pages are created using _hyper text markup language_ , which are a set of special instructions that define how a page will look and specifies the links to other documents.

Once these special instructions, called _tags_ , are added to a document and the document is saved as HTML, it can be viewed as a Web page using a Web browser.

HTML tags, or markups, can be generated by using Web page authoring software specifically designed for this task, or by using Web page authoring features included in many word processing and desktop publishing applications.

Exploring Online

Many Web sites, such as Newbie Help, provide a welcome resource for those new to the Internet and the Web (otherwise known as *newbies*.) Once you have mastered the basics, you can learn how to build your own Web page by visiting pages such as The NCSA Beginner's Guide to HTML and A Basic Home Page, which teach the basics of hypertext markup language (HTML) and Web page design. For more details on basic World Wide Web concepts, visit the Exploring Computers Web page (www.scsite.com/expl.htm) and click World Wide Web.

IV. Web browser software

A *web browser* is a program that displays Web pages and allows users to link to other Web pages.

The first Web browsers used text commands and displayed only text documents. In 1993, however, Mark Andreesen created a Web browser called Mosaic that displayed documents with graphics and used a graphical interface. Mosaic contributed to the rapid growth of the Internet by making it easier and more enjoyable to view Web documents. Andreesen later became one of the founders of Netscape Communications Corporation, a leading Internet software company.

Two of the more common Web browsers are Microsoft Internet Explorer and Netscape Navigator. To view Web pages, a Web browser connects to an Internet computer through an Internet access provider.

The more frequently used Web browser features that are available on the toolbar include:

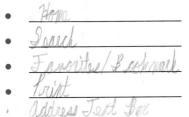

- *Back & forward*
- *Stop*
- *Refresh*
- *Home*

- *Home*
- *Search*
- *Favorites/Bookmark*
- *Print*
  Address Text Box

A. Each time a Web browser is launched, a Web page called a *Home Page* is retrieved and displayed. This page typically is the Web page of the Internet access provider or the manufacturer of the browser.

Although the term, home page, often is used to describe the first page at a Web site, the first page technically is called the Welcome page.

The Web browser home page often provides a quick way to learn about Internet services, new utilities or services, or Internet related news.

Exploring Windows 95

Microsoft uses the World Wide Web to provide regular updates to the Windows 95 operating system. These updates are files that add various functions and features to the operating system, such as device drivers, support tools, mini-applications, utilities, *toys*, and more. The Windows 95 updates are available free from the Microsoft software library on the Web. Once you are connected to the Internet, you can browse through the Windows 95 updates and download files to your computer.

B. A Web page is retrieved using a _Uniform Resource Locator_ , which is an address of a Web page on the Internet.

A URL can specify a:

- _Web site_
- _Document_
- _Part of a doc._

The URL displays in the Address box of the Web browser. All Web page URLs begin with _HTTP_ (hypertext transfer protocol), the communications standard for transferring pages on the Web.

The basic elements of a URL are shown in Figure 12.

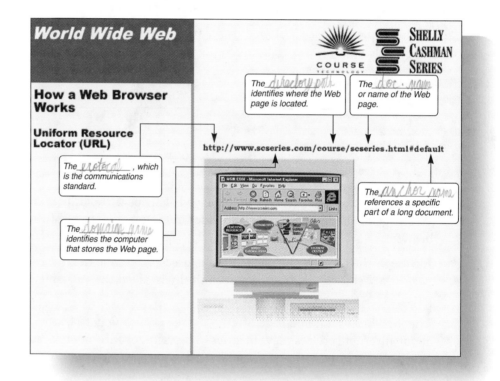

World Wide Web

How a Web Browser Works

Uniform Resource Locator (URL)

The _directory path_ identifies where the Web page is located.

The _doc . name_ or name of the Web page.

http://www.scseries.com/course/scseries.html#default

The _protocol_ , which is the communications standard.

The _domain name_ identifies the computer that stores the Web page.

The _anchor name_ references a specific part of a long document.

Figure 12

Some browsers display the URL of a hyperlinked document at the bottom of the screen. The document can be displayed by clicking the hyperlink or typing the URL in the Location text box of the Web browser. Some browsers change the color of a text hyperlink after it is clicked.

C. Web page URLs can be stored in a favorites or bookmark list. A bookmark consists of the title of a Web page and the URL of that page. A Web page can be retrieved by clicking the _favorites_ button and then simply selecting it from the list.

D. A Web browser keeps track of the Web pages viewed from the moment the browser is launched to when it is exited. The _back and forward buttons_ can be used to revisit pages that have been viewed. Web pages also can be printed directly from the Web browser using the _print button_ .

> ### Exploring Your Computer
>
> Does your computer have a Web browser? If so, which one? Is it the latest version of that particular browser? Have you created any bookmarks in your Bookmarks or Favorites list? Is the Exploring Computers Web page in your bookmarks list?

E. The _stop button_ interrupts the loading of a Web page. The _Refresh button_ is used to reload a Web page from its Web site. The Refresh button might be used with pages that update frequently or to continue loading a Web page after the Stop button has been clicked.

F. Because the Web contains thousands of Web sites on a wide variety of topics, finding information on a specific subject can be difficult. Several companies have created sites with organized directories of Web pages and keyword search capabilities. The _search button_ displays many of the more popular search sites.

V. Search tools

A search tool, also called a _search engine_ , is a program that finds Web sites, Web pages, and Internet files that match keywords. Some search tools look for simple word matches and others allow for more specific searches on a series of words or an entire phrase. The search engine searches an index of Internet sites and documents that is constantly being revised and updated.

The two general types of search tools are:

- _directories_ that organize related Web resources by type.

- _key word_ search programs that find Web pages and files that match specified key words.

Most search sites with directories organize Web pages into categories such as sports, entertainment, or business.

Some popular search tools are Yahoo!, Infoseek, Lycos, AltaVista, Excite, WebCrawler, Four11, and BigBook.

Evaluating the **Results**

True/False

Instructions: Circle **T** if the statement is true or **F** if the statement is false.

T F 1. The World Wide Web is a collection of documents at various locations, called Web sites, all over the world.

T **F** 2. Hypertext documents link text, video, graphics, and sound.

T F 3. Web pages are created using hypertext markup language (HTML).

T F 4. A Web page is retrieved using a Uniform Resource Locator, or URL.

T **F** 5. All Web page URLs begin with WWW, which stands for World Wide Web, the communications standard for transferring pages on the Web.

Matching

Instructions: Write the letter of a description from the column on the right in front of each term in the column on the left.

_g_ 1. Forward and Back buttons

_e_ 2. Stop button

_d_ 3. Refresh button

_a_ 4. Home button

_b_ 5. Favorites button

a. retrieves a designated opening page

b. stores locations of preferred pages

c. displays tools for searching the Web

d. reloads the current Web page

e. interrupts a transmission

f. prints all or a portion of a Web page

g. moves through viewed pages

Multiple Choice

Instructions: Circle the correct response.

1. What type of hyperlink moves from one location in a document to another location within the same document?
   a. target hyperlink
   b. relative hyperlink
   c. absolute hyperlink
   d. all of the above

2. What are two of the more commonly used Web browsers?
   a. Microsoft Internet Explorer and Netscape Navigator
   b. Microsoft Word and Corel WordPerfect
   c. Microsoft Excel and Corel Quattro Pro
   d. Microsoft Access and Paradox

3. What can be specified by a URL?
   a. a Web site
   b. a document on a Web site
   c. a part of a document on a Web site
   d. all of the above

4. What function is performed by the domain name in a URL?
   a. it specifies the communications standard
   b. it references a specific part of a long document
   c. it identifies the computer that stores the Web page
   d. it is the name of the Web page

5. Which button on the toolbar of a Web browser displays many popular tools used to locate information?
   a. Search
   b. Favorites
   c. Home
   d. Refresh

Fill in the Blanks

Instructions: Place the correct word(s) in the blank in each sentence.

1. Web page links are called _hyperlinks_ because they are used to move quickly from one document to another on various Web sites.

2. Jumping from one Web page to another is called _surfing_.

3. A(n) _web browser_ is a program that displays Web pages and allows you to link to other Web pages.

4. A(n) _search engine tool_ is a program that locates Web sites.

5. One general type of search tool is a(n) _directory_, which organizes related Web resources by type.

Examining the **Issues**

1. Web advertisements are in basically two forms: a company's own Web site, or ad space on someone else's. Web advertising is expensive — the cost to reach 1,000 consumers with a thirty-second television spot is about $5.42, while the cost to reach 1,000 consumers with a one-month ad on an online magazine home page is about $75.00. Nevertheless, promoters point out two advantages to advertising on the Web:

   - Unlike a passive television audience, Web consumers make an effort to view an advertisement, actually clicking a hyperlink to visit a company's Web site.

   - Web users tend to be desirable consumers — students and highly educated individuals with median incomes of about $55,000.

   What type of products would benefit most from advertising on the Web? Why? How can advertisers encourage people to return to their Web site? Will Web advertising ever rival television, newspaper, or magazine advertisements? Why or why not?

2. In 1871, a Wells Fargo Wanted poster helped send Black Bart to prison for highway robbery. Once an adornment of bank and post office walls, Wanted posters today have found a new venue—the World Wide Web. Wells Fargo Bank has set up a Web site with small photographs of criminal suspects. Clicking one of the photo hyperlinks displays a larger picture, the reward offered (from $1,000 to $5,000), and a description of the crime. Some law enforcement agencies also are using the Web as a crime-fighting tool. The FBI has posted its 10 Most Wanted on a Web site since 1995. The success of these Web sites is not known, but one of the FBI's Internet posters may have led to the arrest of a bank robber in Guatemala when a 14-year old recognized the suspect as a family friend who helped him hook up his modem. What are the advantages of putting Wanted posters on Web sites? What are the disadvantages? How else might the Web be used to combat crime?

Investigating the World

1. Search engines constantly send out software *spiders* to canvas more than 80 million Web sites, reporting back information that is integrated into indexes. These indexes are combed whenever someone types in a key-word, and the results are displayed in seconds. Unfortunately, a typical query might return almost 50,000 replies. Although ranked by relevancy, locating the most suitable resource still can be cumbersome. A query about the nesting habits of cardinals may return sites having to do with Arizona's football team or prelates of the Catholic Church. Still, considering that the average Internet query is just over one word (queries from professional information seekers — academics and librarians — average about fourteen words), the success of search engines is remarkable. The engineering head of one search tool attributes this success to "wizardry and witchcraft." Think of a topic in which you are interested. Use two different search engines to find information about your topic. Which search engine worked better? Why? How were the returns similar? How were they different? What can a user do to make a search engine more effective?

2. For years, Netscape Navigator dominated Web browsers with a market share from 70% to 85%. Now, however, Microsoft's Internet Explorer is making its presence felt. By borrowing many of Netscape Navigator's features, being a part of the popular Windows 95 operating system, and becoming the browser automatically supplied to America Online's 10 million users, Microsoft's Web browser has seized its own share of the browser market. Which browser is best? Talk to software vendors or users about at least two different Web browsers. How are they similar? How are they different? What are the advantages of each? If possible, try each browser and form your own opinion on their relative merits. Which Web browser would you be more likely to buy? Why?

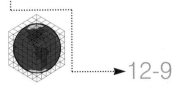

Evaluating Operating Systems

Summarizing the Lab

Instructions: Use the *Evaluating Operating Systems* interactive lab to complete the following outline.

I. What is an operating system?

System Software is a special collection of software that controls the operation of the computer hardware. The _Operating System_ (OS) is the primary component of the system software.

The role of the operating system is illustrated in Figure 13.

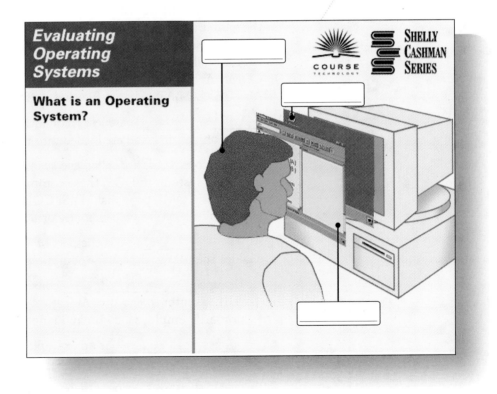

Evaluating Operating Systems

COURSE TECHNOLOGY

SHELLY CASHMAN SERIES

What is an Operating System?

Figure 13

System software frees application software from having to handle tasks that are common among almost all programs that process data. Functions performed by system software include: starting up the computer; loading, executing, and storing application programs; storing and retrieving files; formatting disks; and sorting data files. The three major categories of system software are operating systems, utilities (programs that perform specific tasks related to managing computer resources or files), and language translators (programs used to convert programming instructions into machine language the computer can understand).

II. Parts of an operating system

An operating system consists of several parts: _kernel_ , _External commands_ , and _User interface_ .

A. The _kernel_ contains the most essential and frequently used commands in the operating system, which are called internal commands. When the computer is started, the kernel is _booted_ , or loaded, from the computer's hard disk into memory.

The kernel also is called the *resident* portion of the operating system. When the computer is turned on, the BIOS (Basic Input/Output System), a set of instructions stored in a read only memory (ROM) chip, performs a series of tests. The BIOS then searches for the operating system, starting with drive A and then going to drive C (usually the hard drive). When it locates the operating system, it loads the kernel into memory. In the DOS operating system, the kernel loads the files called CONFIG.SYS (system configuration information), COMMAND.COM (the command language interpreter), and AUTOEXEC.BAT (a batch file that performs optional tasks).

B. _External commands_ are less frequently used commands that remain on the disk and are loaded into memory only as needed.

External commands are called the *nonresident* portion of the operating system. In DOS, these commands include format disk (FORMAT.COM), copy disk (DISKCOPY.COM), and check disk (CHKDSK.COM) as well as many others.

C. A _User interface_ is the part of an operating system that enables the user to access the computer's features.

1. Using a _command language_ consists of typing instructions for the computer to execute. A _command line_ interface primarily employs a command language.

   DOS is an example of a command-line interface.

Some experienced computer operators feel a command-line interface is the fastest, most efficient way to perform certain tasks. Because of the large number of application programs written to work with MS-DOS, it is the operating system on many PCs in the United States. Many applications that work with MS-DOS actually use a menu-driven interface that allows users to select commands from on-screen lists.

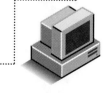

2. With a _graphical user_ (GUI) interface, the user interacts with the computer using a pointing device via graphical representations of the computer's resources.

   Windows 95 is an example of a graphical interface.

   Graphical interfaces are intuitive (easy to use), consistent (the same for different applications), and user-friendly (simple to learn and forgiving of mistakes). To work efficiently, however, they require faster processors, greater disk space, and more memory than command-line interfaces. Improved hardware has addressed many of these difficulties, and the popularity of graphical interfaces continues to grow.

Prior versions of Windows (Windows 3.1 and earlier) were not actually operating systems but operating environments used with DOS that put a graphical interface on a command-line operating system.

> **Exploring Your Computer**
>
> Is your computer running Windows 3.1 or the Windows 95 operating system? If it is Windows 3.1, you are running the DOS operating system under the Windows graphical user interface. Windows 95 is a true operating system, and DOS is no longer required.

III. Functions of operating systems

The operating system enables users and applications to interact with the _computer hardware_.

The main functions of an operating system are _system resource management_, _inter-process management_, and _file management & security_.

A. While using an application program, the operating system manages the use of _computer hardware_ to ensure that it is used correctly.

   System resource management — allocating or assigning the resources of the computer system — is the primary function of the operating system.

   1. In a system where more than one program may run at one time, the operating system manages the sharing of the _CPU's_ time among the various programs. Each program gets a _time slice_, which is a portion of CPU time.

      A time slice usually is measured in milliseconds (thousandths of a second). Unless the system has a heavy work load, users may not even be aware when one program is set aside. The number of time slices given can be adjusted automatically or based on user-specified criteria.

   2. The operating system assigns _memory_ (which may contain data being read or written, instructions to be executed,

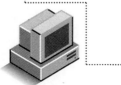

or data waiting to be processed) in several ways to maximize its use.

The operating system transfers the contents of _buffers_, areas of memory that contain data read from or written to an I/O device, to applications that request it. The operating system also assigns memory to _programs_, reallocating unused memory and tracking how much is available.

Operating systems allocate at least some portion of memory into fixed areas called partitions, to which programs and data are assigned. Memory management programs in the OS can alter the size of partitions to accommodate programs and data.

Virtual memory management increases the effective, or *virtual*, limits of memory by expanding the amount of memory to include disk space. The OS transfers sections of data and program instructions, called pages, to and from memory and disk as required.

3. The operating system manages the flow of data to and from _applications_ and controls which applications may access which devices.

Because input and output devices use different commands and control codes to transmit and receive data, the operating system uses programs called device drivers to control these devices. Device drivers usually are supplied with the OS or by the device manufacturers.

B. Many applications split their work into separate tasks, or _threads_, each of which uses a different resource, thus increasing performance. When one thread needs to communicate with another, it signals the _OS_ which in turn notifies the other thread. The operating system also may support passing _data_ between programs.

C. When an application needs to open a _file_ for reading or writing, it requests access through the operating system. The operating system also may keep files secure by preventing unauthorized programs or users from accessing them.

Functions related to file and disk management include formatting hard disks and floppy disks, deleting files, copying files, and renaming files.

To insure file security, most multiuser operating systems employ a logon code that designates the application being used, a user ID that names the user, and a password that authenticates, through its confidentiality, the user's identity. All three items must be entered correctly before files can be accessed.

IV. Types of operating systems

Different kinds of operating systems have been designed to match the features and complexity of different computer architectures.

A. _Single tasking_ operating systems handle only one person using one program at a time.

DOS is an example of a single program operating system.

Single program operating systems were the first type of OS developed. Microsoft Corporation developed both PC-DOS (Personal Computer Disk Operating System) for IBM personal computers and MS-DOS (Microsoft Disk Operating System) for IBM-compatible PCs in 1981.

B. _Task switching_ enhance single program operating systems by automatically swapping programs in and out of memory to allow smooth transitions between them.

Dosshell and the _Windows 3.1_ operating environment are popular examples of task switchers.

A shell program acts as an interface between the user and the operating system, offering a limited number of utility functions.

Exploring Windows 95

The Windows 95 operating system is the much-anticipated successor to Microsoft's Windows 3.1 operating environment. Some of the advantages Windows 95 offers over Windows 3.1 are pre-emptive multitasking that takes advantage of 32-bit microprocessors, Plug-and-Play for adding hardware devices, and a new _desktop_ graphical user interface.

C. _Cooperative Multitasking_ operating systems enable several programs to run simultaneously, with varying degrees of effectiveness.

Although the CPU is capable of working on only one program instruction at a time, its ability to switch back and forth between programs makes it appear that all programs are running at the same time.

1. In a _cooperative_ multitasking system, CPU access is controlled by the programs being used.

   Mac System 7 is a cooperative multitasking system.

   The Macintosh operating system was the first commercially successful graphical user interface when it was released in 1984. It has set the standard for ease of use and has been the model for most other graphical interfaces.

2. In a _pre-emptive_ multitasking system, the operating system has complete control over which program uses the CPU and for how long.

   Highly interactive programs are considered _foreground_ jobs and get more CPU time. Low-priority tasks are _background_ jobs and get less CPU time.

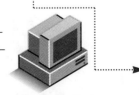

UNIX , _Windows 95_ , and OS/2 are examples of pre-emptive multitasking systems.

UNIX, developed by AT&T, is considered the most portable OS because it can be used with many different types of computers. Unlike Windows 3.1, Windows 95 is a true operating system that does not require DOS. Windows 95 can run programs written for DOS and earlier versions of Windows. OS/2 provides a graphical interface and can run programs written for OS/2, DOS, and Windows.

Although multitasking operating systems on PCs usually support a single user running multiple programs, some multitasking operating systems, called timesharing or multiuser operating systems, can support more than one user running more than one program.

Exploring Online

A host of Web pages discuss, illustrate, and promote various computer operating systems. Yahoo!, for example, lists the URLs of operating system Web sites dedicated to MS-DOS, Windows 95, Windows NT, OS/2, Mac OS, UNIX, and more. For more information on the features of different operating systems, visit the Exploring Computers Web page (www.scsite.com/exl.htm) and click Operating Systems.

D. In computers with more than one CPU (called multiprocessors), a _multiprocessing_ operating system coordinates the CPUs, and maximizes their performance.

High end workstation and _main frames_ are examples of multiprocessing systems.

Multiprocessing is implemented in two ways. In asymmetric multiprocessing, application tasks are assigned to a specific CPU, each of which has its own amount of memory. In symmetric multiprocessing, application tasks may be assigned to whatever CPU is available, and memory is shared among the CPUs.

E. A _virtual machine_ operating system uses the computer hardware to simulate several virtual computers, each of which can run a different operating system. This allows software written for many different operating systems to be run on one computer.

With a virtual machine operating system, different operating systems can be run at the same time, and an appropriate OS can be assigned to each task. System resources are allocated to each operating system. VM is IBM's virtual machine operating system.

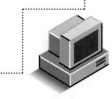

Evaluating the Results

True/False

Instructions: Circle **T** if the statement is true or **F** if the statement is false.

T (F) 1. The entire operating system usually is stored in the computer's memory.

T (F) 2. Data read from or written to an I/O device, such as a disk drive, is stored in areas of memory called threads.

(T) **F** 3. When an application program needs to open a file on disk for reading or writing, it requests access through the operating system.

T (F) 4. In a pre-emptive multitasking system, low priority tasks, such as feeding characters to a printer, are given more CPU time and are considered foreground jobs.

T (F) 5. High-end workstations and mainframes are examples of single program operating systems.

Matching

Instructions: Write the letter of a description from the column on the right in front of each term in the column on the left.

_d_ 1. Single program operating systems

_a_ 2. Task switching operating systems

_g_ 3. Multitasking operating systems

_b_ 4. Multiprocessing operating systems

_e_ 5. Virtual machine operating systems

a. automatically swap programs in and out of memory to allow smooth transitions

b. coordinate the CPUs in compouters that have more than one CPU

c. convert the instructions written by programmers into instructions a computer can understand

d. can handle only one person using one program at a time

e. use the computer hardware to simulate several computers that can each run a different OS

f. consist of programs that tell a computer how to produce information

g. enable several programs to run simultaneously with varying degrees of effectiveness

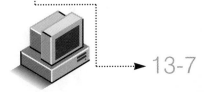

Multiple Choice

Instructions: Circle the correct response.

1. What part of the operating system is booted, or loaded into memory when the computer is started?
   a. utility programs
   b. the supervisor or kernel
   c. external commands
   d. the user interface

2. Which of the following is *not* a function of operating systems?
   a. application program development
   b. system resource management
   c. inter-process communication
   d. file management and security

3. MS-DOS is an example of what type of operating system?
   a. single program
   b. multitasking
   c. multiprocessing
   d. virtual machine

4. What is an example of a cooperative multitasking operating system?
   a. Microsoft Windows 95
   b. UNIX
   c. Macintosh System 7
   d. IBM's OS/2

5. What is the advantage of a virtual machine operating system?
   a. a non-cooperative program cannot keep control of the system until it is finished
   b. many jobs may run in the background without any loss in reaction time
   c. if one CPU fails, work is shifted to the remaining processors
   d. software written for many different operating systems can be run on the same computer

Fill in the Blanks

Instructions: Place the correct word(s) in the blank in each sentence.

1. The primary component of system software is known as the _OS_ .

2. The nonresident portions of the operating system, called _external commands_ are used less frequently and remain on disk until they are needed.

3. Using a(n) _computer language_ interface consists primarily of typing instructions for the computer to execute, such as listing the files on a disk.

4. In a system where more than one program may run at one time, the operating system gives each program a(n) _a time slice_ , which is a portion of CPU time.

5. In a(n) _pre-emptive_ multitasking system, the operating system has complete control over which program uses the CPU and for how long.

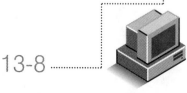

Examining the **Issues**

1. Operating systems can be proprietary (limited to a certain model of computer) or portable (capable of running on many manufacturers' computers). Imagine you are the CEO of Computers and Advanced Technology (CAT), a company that specializes in laptop computers (company slogan: *Life is better with a CAT on your lap*). Your research department has developed an operating system that promises to make most other operating systems seem antiquated. Although designed to work specifically with CAT laptop computers, your programmers assure you the new operating system can be adapted to work with other computers. As CEO, you now have a decision to make. Should the new operating system remain proprietary, so that it only can be used with CAT computers, or should it be made portable, thus making it available to a wider spectrum of users? Explain your decision.

2. Manufacturers often release new versions of operating systems as they continue to make improvements. These versions typically are indicated by numbers following the operating system's name, such as MS-DOS 6.2, with whole numbers marking a major release and decimal numbers denoting minor updates. New releases are generally downwardly compatible, meaning that applications designed to work with earlier versions of the operating system will also work with the later version. For example, a word processing program designed to work with MS-DOS 3.3 will probably work with MS-DOS 6.2. Why are operating systems usually downwardly compatible? What are the advantages of downward compatibility?

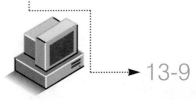

Investigating the World

1. Find out which operating system is used on your or a friend's personal computer. Refer to the documentation that accompanied the operating system to determine what company manufactures the operating system, the operating system's version and release number, and the year it was produced. If possible, find out when the first version of the operating system was introduced, when the next version is expected, and how much is charged for upgrades. Describe the operating system. What kind of interface does it use? How does it perform system resource management, inter-process communication, and file management and security? What type of operating system is it? In general, what do you like about the operating system? What do you dislike?

2. Most application software (such as word processing, desktop publishing, spreadsheet, database, presentation graphics, communications, electronic mail, personal information management, project management, or games) are written for a specific operating system. Visit a store that sells computer software and make a list of at least five applications you would like to have on your personal computer. Find out the name of the operating system with which each of the applications you selected is designed to work. If an application does not work with the same operating system as the others, try to locate a similar one that does. Your goal is to find five applications that work with the same operating system. List the final five you choose and note the operating system they all use. What features, if any, did you have to give up to find five applications that use the same operating system?

Working at Your Computer

Summarizing the Lab

Instructions: Use the *Working at Your Computer* interactive lab to complete the following outline.

I. Working at the computer

As people spend more time working at computers, _correct posture_ while working is becoming increasingly important.

Incorrect posture can lead to _pain_ and _repetitive stress injuries_ and can cause permanent physical damage.

Good posture at the computer depends on two things:

- _user awareness_
- _good computer workstation_

A key characteristic of a well-designed workplace is flexibility. The workplace should be able to accommodate different sizes and tastes, to *custom fit* each worker.

II. What is ergonomics?

Ergonomics is an _applied science_ that studies people's physical and cognitive characteristics in order to effectively design and arrange the things people use. Ergonomics can be used to design a _workstation_ that properly positions a person's body in relation to the computer.

Ergonomics is sometimes called *human engineering*. About three decades ago, automobile manufacturers discovered they could boost sales by using ergonomics to design cars that were comfortable for drivers and passengers. In a similar way, an ergonomically designed workplace can raise productivity by minimizing fatigue and increasing worker satisfaction.

> ### Exploring Online
>
> Agile Corporation's Ergonomics Home Page and Intergraph Corporation's Ergonomics Office Guide are devoted to computer ergonomics.
>
> Yahoo! also lists a variety of online companies that provide ergonomic accessories to make working at your computer safer and more comfortable. To learn more ways to improve working at your computer, visit the Exploring Computers Web page (www.scsite.com/expl.htm) and click Ergonomics.

III. Good posture

The goal of good posture is _balance_ and _ease of movement_.

Good posture is achieved when the weight of the body is supported by the _spine_, and the _muscles_ provide lateral support.

Back, neck, or shoulder pain, the leading causes of lost work time, can all result from poor posture.

A. Ideally, sit with the _back_ upright but not tense. The contour of the _chair_ should follow the slight natural curve of the lower back.

Slumping or leaning forward causes _lower back pain_.

If it is frequently necessary to use a telephone and computer at the same time, a telephone headset should be considered. Cradling a phone between the shoulder and neck can cause muscle strain.

B. The _head_ should be right above the shoulders so that the spine can support its weight. The monitor should be placed so the top of the screen is at _eye level_.

The angle from the eyes down to the center of the screen should be about 20°.

Leaning the head back to look at the screen can _strain your muscles_ and cause _headaches_.

An adjustable monitor is recommended, and the screen should be tilted ±7° off perpendicular. The monitor should be about an arm's length away from the body. To minimize strain, a document holder that grips printed material next to the computer screen can be attached to the monitor or placed on your desk.

C. When working at the computer, both _shoulders_ should be back and relaxed. The distance between the _keyboard_ and the upper body should be small enough so that it is not necessary to lean forward.

Leaning forward or working with one shoulder pushed forward can lead to muscle strain in the _sholder & neck_.

It is recommended that users stand up and walk around once each hour, and take at least a fifteen minute break every two hours.

D. The _forearm_ should be parallel with the ground, allowing the wrist and hand to float over the keyboard. The angle between the forearm and upper arm will be _90°_.

The most commonly reported problems associated with prolonged keyboard use are called repetitive stress injury (RSI) or cumulative trauma disorder (CTD). Government statistics indicate these injuries are responsible for half of all work-related illnesses.

1. Office desks often are too high for using a keyboard or mouse, forcing the forearm to be angled upward and wrist to arch, which strains the _muscles & tendons_.

   If the desk is too high, the keyboard can be lowered by attaching a _keyboard tray_ to the bottom of the desk, or the _chair_ can be raised to achieve the proper angle for the forearm.

2. Resting the _wrist_ on a surface while typing causes _dorsiflexion_, or the upward tilting of the hand toward the arm, which is a major source of injuries.

   Ideally, the keyboard should be _flat_ on the desk, or even raised in front.

3. The hands should be placed in a _neutral forward_ position while typing. Pushing the hands to either side can _strain your muscles_ and cause injuries.

   Sufferers of carpal tunnel syndrome (CTS), a specific type of RSI, complain of weakness and pain in their wrists and hands and have difficulty grasping objects. CTS injuries are caused by pressure on the median nerve in the wrist, and can be permanently disabling.

dorsiflexion
flat
neutral forward

Exploring Windows 95

The Microsoft Natural keyboard, designed specifically for Windows 95, is an ergonomically sound device that includes a built in wrist-rest below the keys themselves. The wrist-rest promotes good wrist positioning by raising the wrist to the same level as the hand and reducing dorsiflexion.

E. The angle between the spine and the thighs should be at least _90°_. The thighs should slope _slightly downward_, and the feet should rest _flat on the floor_, helping to keep the back in an upright position.

hips
footrest

When sitting correctly, the weight of the body rests on the
hips . If the chair is too high, a *foot rest*
can be used to keep the body in the correct alignment.

Getting out and taking a walk at lunch can provide exercise and help
to relieve stress.

IV. Protecting your eyes

Looking at the *computer screen* can be stressful to the eyes. Two
ergonomic factors can alleviate eyestrain: *lighting* and
distance from computer screen

A. The key to proper lighting is to make sure there is no *glare*
on the computer screen. Locating the screen *perpendicular*
to light sources and away from overhead lights minimizes reflected
light.

Perpendicular

Glare can be reduced by: putting a *cover* above the
monitor, using an *anti-glare filter*, and keeping the
screen clean .

screen clean

Ideally, the screen should be three to four times brighter than the
room.

B. To minimize eyestrain, the distance from the eyes to the computer
screen should be *18 to 28"* .

18 to 28 in.

The correct relationship between the body and the computer workstation is illustrated in Figure 14.

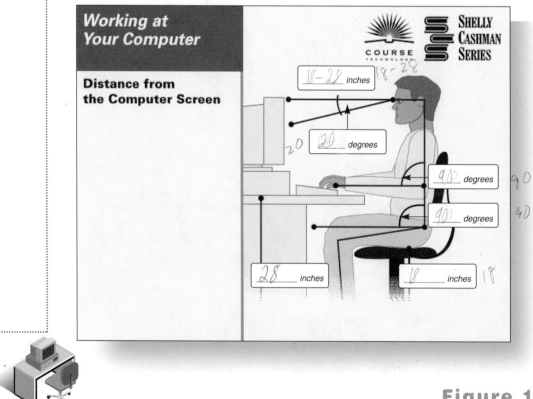

**Working at
Your Computer**

**Distance from
the Computer Screen**

COURSE TECHNOLOGY

**SHELLY
CASHMAN
SERIES**

18-28 inches   *18-28*

20   *20* degrees

90 degrees   *90*

90 degrees   *40*

28 inches

18 inches   *18*

Figure 14

Workplace health considerations also should include the type and volume of work. People in stressful jobs need frequent breaks, and those who enter large amounts of data need regular breaks that incorporate hand and wrist exercises. Workers also can reduce tension and anxiety by eliminating or minimizing surrounding noise.

Computer users should be aware of the symptoms of repetitive stress injuries (soreness, pain, numbness, or weakness in the neck, shoulders, arms, wrists, or hands) and seek medical advice if these symptoms are experienced.

Exploring Your Computer

Take a minute to evaluate how you work at your computer. Are you seated comfortably, with good posture? Are your hands and arms in the proper position? Is your work area well lit? These are all important factors in creating a comfortable work environment and reducing the risk of computer-related injuries.

Evaluating the Results

True/False

Instructions: Circle **T** if the statement is true or **F** if the statement is false.

T F 1. The goal of good posture is balance and ease of movement.

T **F** 2. Working with one shoulder pushed forward can reduce muscle strain in the shoulder and neck.

T F 3. Desks used in offices often are too high for using a keyboard or mouse, requiring the forearm to be angled upward and the wrist to arch.

T **F** 4. Raising the back edge of the keyboard reduces the problem of dorsiflexion, which is a major source of injuries.

T F 5. If you feel pressure on your tailbone when sitting at the computer, your chair is too high.

Matching

Instructions: Write the letter of a description from the column on the right in front of each term in the column on the left.

_d_ 1. 18 to 28 inches

_b_ 2. 20 degrees

_e_ 3. 28 inches

_a_ 4. 90 degrees

_g_ 5. 18 inches

a. the angle between the forearm and upper arm

b. the angle the screen is tilted off perpendicular

c. the angle from the eyes to the center of the screen

d. the distance from eyes to the screen

e. the distance from the floor to the desktop

f. the distance from elbow to the keyboard

g. the distance from the floor to the chair seat

Multiple Choice

Instructions: Circle the correct response.

1. On what does good posture at the computer depend?
   a. the user's awareness of the proper ways to hold the body while using the computer
   b. proper lighting in the room and a suitable distance from the computer screen to the user
   c. a computer workstation that allows the user to sit and hold the body properly while typing or using the mouse
   d. both a and c

2. How should the monitor be placed?
   a. so the top of the screen is 20° below eye level
   b. so the top of the screen is at eye level
   c. so the top of the screen is 20° above eye level
   d. so the bottom of the screen is at eye level

3. What should be the distance between the keyboard and the upper body?
   a. small enough so that your elbows are well behind your back
   b. small enough so that you do not have to lean forward to reach the keyboard
   c. large enough so that your wrists rest on the desk in front of the keyboard
   d. large enough so that you can fully extend your arms to reach the keyboard

4. Having your legs and feet in the right position will help to keep which of the following in the correct position?
   a. your back
   b. your wrists
   c. your head
   d. your hands

5. What is the key to proper lighting of the work environment?
   a. to make sure the room in which you work is brightly lit
   b. to make sure the computer screen is located close to overhead lights
   c. to make sure there is no glare on the computer screen
   d. to make sure light sources are parallel to the computer screen

Fill in the Blanks

Instructions: Place the correct word(s) in the blank in each sentence.

1. _Ergonomics_ can be used to design a workstation that properly positions a person's body in relation to the computer.

2. Good posture is achieved when the weight of the body is supported by the _spine_ .

3. When working at the computer, your _forearm_ should be parallel with the floor, allowing the wrist and hand to float over the keyboard as you type.

4. Resting the wrists on a surface as you type causes _dorsiflexion_ , or the upward tilting to the hand toward the arm, which is a major source of injuries.

5. A(n) _anti-glare screen_ can help reduce reflected light on the computer screen, although it sometimes makes reading characters on the screen more difficult.

Examining the Issues

1. Once experienced mainly by line workers in poultry processing plants, repetitive stress injury (RSI) is a leading complaint today among computer workers. To date, offices have relied primarily on hardware answers to health concerns — suitable furniture and the proper placement of computer equipment. A product called Bodysavers, however, now offers a software solution. Bodysavers is a screen saver that, when there has been no input for a period of time, displays a message reminding computer users to exercise. Bodysavers also regularly interrupts users to show elementary hand and body stretches. Keeping in mind the cost of the software and the time users would spend not working, do you think Bodysavers would be a wise investment for a large office? Why or why not?

2. The introduction of computers in the workplace can cause not only physical problems, but emotional problems as well. A researcher from International Research Development, Inc. reported that about one-fourth of the work force may have experienced emotional stress related to the use of computers. Established workers described feelings of incompetence, loss of control, job insecurity, and anticipated demotion when computers were introduced in their offices. These feelings, which are sometimes called *compuphobia*, can have a tremendous impact on worker morale and productivity. Why are established workers more likely to experience compuphobia? If you were the manager of an office in which computers were being introduced, what might you do to prevent compuphobia?

Investigating the World

1. Imagine you are a consultant that specializes in workplace ergonomics. Using the information presented in this lab, prepare a checklist that can be used to evaluate a computer workstation. The checklist should contain a list of desirable characteristics and a scale with which each could be rated. Finally, decide on a passing grade for a workstation. After you have finished, visit the computer lab at your installation and use your checklist to evaluate one of the workstations. Did the workstation pass? If not, what has to be done for it to meet your approval? If the workstation was acceptable, how do you think it could be improved?

2. To minimize the risk of carpal tunnel syndrome, several ergonomically designed keyboards have been developed. Visit a computer vendor or use a computer equipment catalog to find at least two ergonomically designed keyboards. Who manufactures each keyboard? In what way are they different from standard keyboards? How do they reduce the chance of wrist injury? If possible, try out the keyboards. Compared to standard keyboards, are they more or less comfortable? Are they easier or more difficult to use? Why? How do the ergonomically designed keyboards compare to standard keyboards in terms of price? If they are more expensive, are they worth it? Why or why not?

Designing a
Database

Summarizing the Lab

15

Instructions: Use the *Designing a Database* interactive lab to complete the following outline.

I. What is a database?

A database is a way of _storing_ a large amount of data to provide easy access.

Effective data management involves data integrity or data accuracy (assuring the reliability of the source and entry of data), data security (protecting data to keep it from being misused or lost), and data maintenance (keeping data current).

Exploring Windows 95

Most personal computer database software applications have versions that take advantage of the features offered by Windows 95. Some of the database packages with versions designed for Windows 95 are:

- Borland Visual dBASE
- Claris FileMaker Pro
- Corel Paradox 7
- Lotus Approach
- Microsoft Access
- Microsoft Visual FoxPro

Each similar item in a database is stored as a _record_ .
Data within each record is divided into areas called _fields_ .

A file is a collection of related data or information. Files are made up of records, which are structured groups of related facts. The individual facts within each record are called fields. The same fields are used in each record in a file.

Data typically is stored as an isolated set called a _flat file_, an independent file that contains all the information necessary to process the records in that file.

Flat files usually are designed for a single application. All the records in a flat file have the same format (the same fields and the same data types).

A database allows users to access and relate data across _multiple files_, rather than restricting a search to a single file.

Because database files are related, records can be processed using information from more than one file. Users can draw information from a database for a variety of purposes in different formats.

Databases offer several advantages over flat files.

- Reduced data redundancy — In a database, shared data elements are stored in a single location.

- Improved data integrity — With a database, data is updated in a single location, so it is more likely to be accurate.

- Easier reporting — A database allows data to be extracted from multiple files at one time.

- Improved data security — One plan can establish different levels of access to the information in a database.

- Reduced development time — In a database, additional data can be accommodated by adding new attributes to existing files.

II. Types of databases

The four main categories of database structure are shown on Figure 15.

A. In a _hierarchical_ database, data is organized in a series of parent-child relationships.

Because a child record can have only one parent, if a child record belongs in two different families _a copy_ must be placed in each one.

Hierarchical databases are the oldest form of database organization. Data stored on lower levels of the hierarchy is accessed through the higher levels. All data relationships are established when the hierarchical database is created. As a result, adding new fields to the database requires the redefinition of the entire database. Because data relationships are predefined, however, access to and updating of data is very fast.

B. A _network_ database is similar to a hierarchical database except that each child record can have more than one parent.

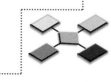

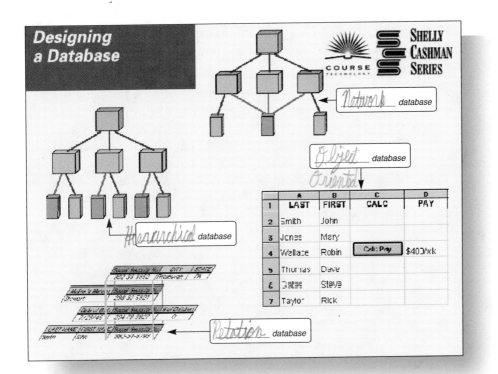

Figure 15

Sharing a child record eliminates _redundancy_ and increases _accessibility_ .

In a network database, parent and child records are referred to as _members_ and _owners_ .

An owner and its one or more associated members is called a set (or owner-coupled set). A member can be accessed through any of its owners. Like a hierarchical database, data relationships must be established before the database is used and must be redefined if fields are added or modified.

C. A _relational_ database links data in multiple files using a single field that is common to each file.

Databases containing different _kinds of data_ can be accessed easily once they are linked using a common field. New fields can be added to one database without affecting the others.

In a relational database, data is organized in tables (called relations), which are further divided into rows (called tuples) and fields (called attributes). Relational databases offer more flexibility than hierarchical or network databases; because data relationships are not predefined, attributes can be added without having to redefine the entire database. Yet, its more complex software requires more powerful computers to provide acceptable performance.

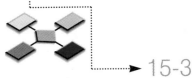

D. An _object oriented_ database stores objects that contain data and the actions that can be taken on that data.

Object-oriented databases are the most adaptable type of database. In hierarchical, network, and relational databases, the same fields are used for each record in a file. A company using one of these database types might need two files to calculate its weekly payroll: one with an hourly rate field for employees paid by the hour, and a second with an annual salary field for salaried employees. Because it allows variations of a single record type, however, records in an object-oriented database can contain many different methods to compute weekly pay.

Exploring Online

Several sites on the Internet provide a comprehensive glossary of database terms, and tips and tricks for good database design. Some excellent database resources on the Web include:

- Data Warehouse Glossary
- University of Massachusetts Database Systems Laboratory
- Association for Computing Machinery's Special Interest Group on Management of Data

For more information on designing a database, visit the Exploring Computers Web page (www.scsite.com/expl.htm) and click Database.

III. Accessing a database

Accessing a database involves entering a request that specifies which data to display.

Two ways to make a query are:

A. _Query by example_ enables the user to build a query step by step. A list of database fields is presented, and the user enters _criteria_ into one or more of the fields. As the user narrows the qualifiers, only the data that matches the choices is displayed.

Users can enter simple expressions in a field (such as Jones in a LASTNAME field to find people whose last names are Jones) or create expressions in a field using relational operators (such as >30 in an AGE field to find people older than thirty). Criteria can be combined using the logical operators, NOT, AND, and OR (for example, Jones in a LASTNAME field AND >30 in an AGE field to find people named Jones who are older than thirty).

B. A _query language_ enables users to describe what data they wish to access using English-like phrases, following the syntax of

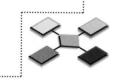

the query language. _Structured Query Language_ or SQL is the most widely used query language.

The American National Standards Institute issued standards for SQL in 1987. Today, most database software has incorporated SQL.

Three operations are used to query a relational database: select (which chooses certain records), project (which specifies the fields, or attributes, that appear on the query output), and join (which combines two files or relations).

IV. Database features

Features in a database management system that help to maintain data include: _data dictionary_ , _utility programs_ , _data security_ , and _data recovery_ .

A. The _data dictionary_ defines how data in the database is organized into fields and helps ensure new data is entered correctly.

Because it contains the structures and specifications for the database, a data dictionary must be carefully designed and documented.

B. _Utility programs_ provide maintenance features, such as copying or deleting records and monitoring the database's performance.

C. _Data security_ features enable the database creators to set various levels of access privileges that determine how different users can interact with the data.

Without some type of access security, data in a database is more subject to unauthorized access than data in a decentralized system of individual files.

D. The _data recovery_ feature tracks changes made to the database. Changes are recorded in a _log_ , which can be used to reconstruct data in the event of accident or malfunction and to reveal patterns of database use.

V. Design guidelines

Carefully designed database files can make it easy for the user to query and report on database information. For relational databases, a process called normalization is used to organize data into the most efficient and logical file relationships.

Designing an efficient and powerful database can be done by following some simple guidelines.

A. Designing a database _on paper_ first provides an overview of the problem and shows how the data should be organized before tackling the details.

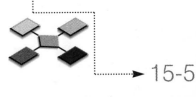

Exploring Your Computer

Sketch one of these simple databases on paper:

- A friend database, with fields for names, addresses, and telephone numbers
- A favorite music group database, with fields for the group's name, group members, and their albums

If you have access to a database program, such as Access or Paradox, create an electronic version of your database, entering at least five records.

B. A _key field_ is used to sort the data in a database. Each record's key field should be _unique_ .

C. Data that can be derived from existing fields in the database is _redundant_ and can be eliminated.

D. If items need to be referred to separately, it is best to keep them in _separate fields_ .

E. Adding _a default value_ , or a value that is usually the same for a particular field, can greatly reduce the time it takes to add new data.

Although formal rules do not exist for designing flat files, the same common sense guidelines can be applied to both databases and flat files.

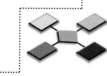

Evaluating the **Results**

True/False

Instructions: Circle **T** if the statement is true or **F** if the statement is false.

T **F** 1. A flat file enables users to access and relate data across multiple files.

T **F** 2. Query by example, or QBE, enables the user to build a query step by step.

T **F** 3. A log can reveal patterns of database use and provide a data trail that can be used to reconstruct a database in the event of an accident or malfunction.

T **F** 4. Each record's key field data should be the same as every other record's key field data.

T **F** 5. Any data that can be derived from existing fields in a database should be entered again in a separate field.

Matching

Instructions: Write the letter of a description from the column on the right in front of each term in the column on the left.

_a_ 1. Query language

_g_ 2. Data dictionary

_f_ 3. Utility program

_e_ 4. Data security

_d_ 5. Data recovery

a. enables users to describe the data they wish to access using English-like phrases

b. combines items containing data with actions that can be taken on the data

c. links multiple files using a single field

d. tracks changes made to the database and records changes in a log

e. enables the database creators to set different levels of access privileges

f. provides maintenance features such as copying or deleting records

g. defines how data in the database is organized into fields

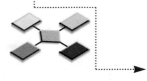

Multiple Choice

Instructions: Circle the correct response.

1. Each similar item in a database is stored as what?
   a. a file
   b. a record
   c. a field
   d. a relation

2. In what type of database is data organized in a series of parent-child relationships?
   a. hierarchical
   b. network
   c. relational
   d. object-oriented

3. In what type of database can new fields be added without affecting the other fields?
   a. hierarchical
   b. network
   c. relational
   d. all of the above

4. What helps to ensure that new data is entered into the database correctly?
   a. a data dictionary
   b. utility programs
   c. data security
   d. data recovery

5. Which of the following is *not* a guideline for designing an efficient and powerful database?
   a. start on paper ✓
   b. use a unique key field ✓
   c. choose default values ✓
   d. maximize data redundancy

Fill in the Blanks

Instructions: Place the correct word(s) in the blank in each sentence.

1. A(n) _database_ is a collection of related files and a way of storing a large amount of data to allow easy access.

2. Data typically is stored in an independent, isolated set called a(n) _flat file_ .

3. In a network database, parent and child records are referred to as _owners_ and members.

4. A(n) _object oriented_ database stores items containing data and the actions that can be taken on that data.

5. _SQL_ is the most widely used query language.

Examining the **Issues**

1. Imagine if, instead of using a central database, your school used a flat file system to handle student records. Basic data (such as your name, address, and telephone number) may be kept in a central office file; financial data would be kept in the school business office file; data concerning your grades may be kept in files by individual instructors; and data on the credits you have earned would be in department and central office files. What would be the disadvantages of this type of system? What might be the advantages?

2. Data security is an important part of managing data. With a database system, data security often involves setting varying access levels for different groups of people. Access levels might include: (1) no access at all; (2) data can be viewed but not changed; (3) some data can be changed but not all; and (4) total access with no restraints. Consider your student file. In addition to your name, address, and grades, this file may contain information on your ethnicity, gender, family, financial status, health, extra-curricular activities, disciplinary record, and so on. Using this file as an example, which of the four levels of access privileges would you give to each of the following groups: you, other students, faculty, administration, and outside organizations. Why?

Investigating the World

1. Automobile dealers often use databases that contain information both about cars in their own inventories and cars in the inventories of related dealers. Most libraries use computerized databases to keep track of their own collections and books in neighboring libraries. Law enforcement agencies use databases to store data on past criminal activity. Visit one of these organizations or another organization that uses a database, and interview the person in charge of the organization's database. How many groups are represented in the database? Who has access to the database? How is the database used? How often is it updated? What are the advantages of using a database? What are the disadvantages?

2. One of the most interesting applications of computerized databases is in the sports arena. Some database programs are designed to help individual athletes, such the Sport Sight program that studies a baseball pitcher's motion or the Sports Technology program that analyzes a golfer's swing. Other programs, such as one from Sports-Tech International, are used by college and professional teams. These programs can help in evaluating players and determining how other teams handle certain situations. The Indiana Pacers credit their database programs in the selection of Kenny Williams in the draft and the defeat of Michael Jordan and the Chicago Bulls in the first six games the teams played after starting the system. Using current magazines and other resources, research the relationship between computerized databases and sports. How are databases being used? How might they be used in the future? What impact will databases have on individual and team sports?

Choosing a Programming Language

16

Summarizing the Lab

Instructions: Use the *Choosing a Programming Language* interactive lab to complete the following outline.

I. What is a programming language?

To communicate with a computer, a person uses a *program language* — a set of written words and symbols that have meaning for the computer.

Programming is the process of writing computer programs, or the instructions that tell a computer what to do. Program development involves five steps: review specifications (define the problem and determine what needs to be done), design (develop a logical solution to the task), code (write the instructions in a programming language), test (check the written instructions to make sure they work), and finalize documentation (complete records that explain the program).

> **Exploring Windows 95**
>
> Programmers designing software for Windows 95 must meet a detailed set of guidelines to receive approval from Microsoft, which allows them to put the *Designed for Windows 95* logo on their products. For example, programs must support long file names and be able to run under Windows NT (another Microsoft operating system) as well as Windows 95.

Each programming language has its own *syntax*, or rules, which must be followed to form meaningful program statements.

Syntax errors missed by a programmer usually are identified by the computer when it decodes the program instructions. Logic errors, which cause the wrong processing to take place, are more difficult to detect. During desk checking, programmers review the logic of a program and try to find errors, called *bugs*. Debugging is the process of locating and correcting program errors.

II. Types of programming languages

Programming languages fall into the categories illustrated in Figure 16.

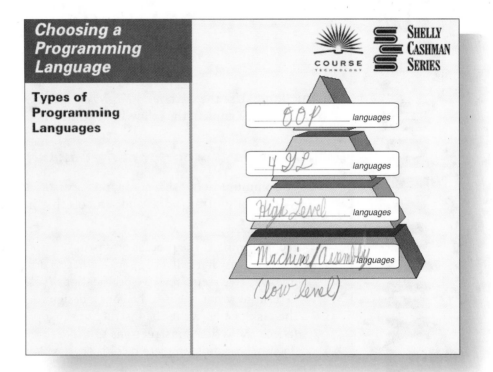

Figure 16

A. <u>Machine language</u> is a computer's native language. It is a series of <u>numbers</u> representing basic operations.

Computers with different processors have different machine languages, because each microprocessor's <u>instruction set</u> is unique.

Programs written in all other language categories are converted into machine language before they are executed.

Machine language can be very efficient because the programmer has direct control over the computer. Nevertheless, machine language programs take a long time to write, are difficult to review for errors, and can run only on specific processors.

B. <u>Assembly language</u> make machine languages easier to remember by assigning text abbreviations to each machine instruction.

An assembler is a special program that converts assembly language programs into machine language.

The abbreviations used in assembly languages are called mnemonics or symbolic operation codes. Assembly languages often include macroinstructions that generate more than one machine language instruction. Like machine languages, assembly languages are machine dependent, which means they can work only with specific hardware.

C. _High level language_ contain nouns and verbs, similar to human languages, to make programming easier.

High-level languages are _machine independent_ meaning that programs written using these languages can be run on many different types of computers.

The *sentences* in high-level language programs are called program statements. Because they are similar to human languages, high-level languages can be read by programmers and are easier to learn and use than machine or assembly languages. Although more advanced languages have been developed, high-level languages remain popular because of the large number of existing programs in which they have been used.

High-level languages are translated into machine languages in two ways: a compiler translates an entire program that is then stored for later execution; or an interpreter translates one program statement at a time, executes it, and then moves on to the next program statement. An interpreter makes it easier to find errors, but takes longer to execute an entire program than a compiler.

D. _Fourth Generation languages_ , or 4GLs, are commonly described as _non procedural_ , meaning that the programmer simply communicates what tasks should be done instead of specifying the steps required to perform them.

4GLs, sometimes called very high-level languages, are described as being results oriented because programmers can specify what is to be done (usually by describing the output) without having to stipulate how it is to be done. Although they provide fewer processing options and require more computer processing power than other language generations, because of their ease of use experts predict 4GLs will continue to be popular.

A natural language, or fifth generation language, is an extension of 4GLs that allows users to enter a query as if speaking to another person.

E. _Object Oriented Programming_ , or OOP, is a new trend in language design that combines data and related instructions into self-contained items called objects.

The instructions contained in an object are called _methods_ . New types of data can re-use, or _inherit_ , the capabilities of existing data types.

An object is part of a class, or group, with specific characteristics. An object inherits all of the methods of its class and also has methods unique to the object. As OOP is used by an organization, the organization builds up a library of OOP objects and classes. Objects can be used in different programs, which significantly reduces programming time. OOP often is described as event-driven, meaning the program responds to events that take place when an application is run and does not have to proceed from beginning to end in a linear manner.

> ### Exploring Online
>
> Yahoo! lists a number of sites related to programming languages such as BASIC, COBOL, C, and more. JavaWorld, by contrast, is an online magazine devoted to Java. To learn more about the programming languages discussed in this chapter, visit the Exploring Computers Web page (www.scsite.com/expl.htm) and click Programming.

III. Application generators

An application generator is a _program builder_ that produces programs in other languages. Users describe the _input_, _processing_, and _output_ desired, and the application generator creates a suitable program. Application generators usually include tools to help programmers easily create _menus_ and _screens_ for the new program.

Application generators, also called program generators, are available as stand-alone programs or as part of other software. They use standard processing modules (such as routines to read, write, or compare records), which are stored in a library and selected and grouped together based on user specifications.

IV. Programming languages used today

Many programming languages have evolved to fulfill a variety of computing needs.

A. _BASIC_, a high-level language designed to be easy for students to learn and use, also is used to develop business and scientific applications. Many computer systems include a customized version of BASIC, such as Microsoft's _Q Basic (QuickBasic)_

BASIC is an easy to use, flexible language that can be used to write programs in almost any area. Most versions of BASIC are interpreted, so programmers are informed of errors instantly. BASIC has become one of the most popular programming languages and is supported by nearly every computer, although different computers may use different versions of BASIC.

B. _COBOL_ , another high-level language used for business applications, is written in sentences and paragraphs, making programs easy to read and understand. COBOL is best suited to performing _simple calculations_ on large amounts of data.

COBOL is widely used, especially on large computers. As companies downsize, PC versions of COBOL have become popular. Some experts believe that COBOL has been used to write more than 75 percent of today's business software. COBOL programs can be up to seven times longer than programs written in other languages, but they are easy to debug and maintain (revise).

C. _FORTRAN_ , the first high-level language, is designed to be used by scientists, engineers, and mathematicians. FORTRAN is noted for its ability to express and calculate _mathmatical equations_ easily.

Although it was developed in the 1950s, FORTRAN is still popular and can be used with almost all computers, including mainframes and personal computers. Because FORTRAN is capable of executing complex formulas, it continues to be widely employed in the scientific community.

D. The _Pascal_ language, developed as a tool for teaching programming, intentionally omits more powerful statements that may be difficult for novice programmers. Due to its highly structured syntax, Pascal encourages students to follow the principles of _structured program .designed_

Structured program design is a methodology that emphasizes professionally accepted standards and logic. These design concepts help to create programs that are easy to write, read, understand, check for errors, and maintain. Because Pascal is an excellent tool for presenting proper programming techniques, it is often a required course for computer science and information systems majors.

E. _C_ , a high-level language originally developed for writing system software, has become widely used on all types of computers. Many _Operating Systems_ and application programs are written in C.

C offers a great deal of flexibility, and C programs are efficient and fast. C is the language preferred by many professionals who write programs for personal computers. Special effects in several films, including *Star Trek*, were developed using C.

F. _C++_ is a version of C enhanced with object-oriented features. Programs written in _C_ can be converted to C++ and modified to take advantage of its additional features.

Like C, C++ is a powerful and efficient language but it can be difficult to learn. Object-oriented programming requires a different approach from procedural programming, and traditional programmers sometimes have trouble using the object-oriented characteristics of C++. Despite this, C++ is used frequently to develop application software.

G. _Visual Language_ enable programmers to create graphical, object-oriented programs for the Windows environment. These languages feature object-oriented tools and help programmers build _graphical User interface_ into their programs. _GUI_

H. _Java_ is a simple object-oriented programming language developed by Sun Microsystems that can be used to develop programs able to be delivered over the Internet. For example, Java programs called _Applet_ can be included in a Web page and viewed or downloaded using a Web browser.

Other commonly used programming languages include HyperTalk (Apple's object-oriented language), LISP and Prolog (fourth-generation languages used for artificial intelligence applications), Ada (the language used by the defense department), LOGO (an educational tool used with small children), PL/1 (a language that combines features of COBOL and FORTRAN), and RPG (a language developed to simplify production of business reports).

Exploring Your Computer

Your computer runs a variety of programs written in a various programming languages. For example, both Microsoft and Lotus have developed application software using C. *Exploring Computers*, the program that is currently running on your computer, was developed using Macromedia Director, a multimedia authoring program written in C++.

V. Choosing a language

Choosing a language for the solution to a programming task depends on many factors: _Standards_ , _Communication_ , _Suitability_ , and _Portability_ .

A. The organization that will use the new program may have a _standard_ specifying the language used for all programs.

B. A new program must be able to _communicate_ efficiently with existing programs, which may be easier if all programs are written in the same language.

C. Different programming languages are better _suited_ to solving some problems than others.

D. _Portability_ is the ability to run a program on different computer platforms without modification.

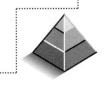

A final consideration is the expertise of available programmers. Unless another language is far superior, it is best to choose a language with which programmers are comfortable.

Evaluating the Results

True/False

Instructions: Circle **T** if the statement is true or **F** if the statement is false.

T (**F**) 1. As computers have become more sophisticated, programming languages have become less user-friendly.

T (**F**) 2. Computers with different processors have the same machine language because all processors have identical instruction sets.

T (**F**) 3. High-level languages commonly are described as machine-dependent, meaning that a program written in a high-level language can be run on only one type of computer.

(**T**) **F** 4. In the traditional programming model, data and the instructions that operate on the data are kept separate.

(**T**) **F** 5. With OOP, new types of data can re-use, or inherit, the capabilities of existing data types.

Matching

Instructions: Write the letter of a description from the column on the right in front of each term in the left column on the left.

___f___ 1. BASIC

___e___ 2. COBOL

___a___ 3. Java

___g___ 4. Pascal

___d___ 5. C

a. an object-oriented language, used to write programs for delivery over the Internet

b. a fourth-generation language used with artificial intelligence applications

c. a high-level language best suited to performing simple calculations on large amounts of data

d. a high-level language originally designed for writing system software

e. a high-level language designed to simplify the preparation of business reports

f. a high-level language designed to be easy for students to learn and use

g. a highly structured language developed as a tool for teaching programming

Multiple Choice

Instructions: Circle the correct response.

1. Into what language must all programs be translated before they run?
   a. machine language
   b. assembly language
   c. high-level language
   d. fourth-generation language

2. How is object-oriented programming different from traditional programming?
   a. instructions are arranged in sentences and grouped into paragraphs
   b. programmers must specify the procedures used to accomplish a task
   c. data and related instructions are combined into self-contained items
   d. abbreviations are used to represent machine operation code

3. What language intentionally omits program statements that may be difficult for novice programmers and encourages students to follow the principles of structured program design?
   a. FORTRAN
   b. Pascal
   c. COBOL
   d. C

4. What are visual languages?
   a. languages that display all necessary characters and symbols on the computer screen
   b. languages that use lines between program statements to illustrate relationships
   c. languages that help programmers build graphical user interfaces into their programs
   d. languages that show the result of a program statement immediately after it is entered

5. Which of the following is *not* a factor in choosing a programming language?
   a. the necessity for the application to be portable
   b. the programming standards of the organization
   c. the need to isolate new programs from existing programs
   d. the suitability to the application being programmed

Fill in the Blanks

Instructions: Place the correct word(s) in the blank in each sentence.

1. A(n) *programming language* is a set of written words and symbols that have meaning for the computer.

2. Each programming language has its own *syntax*, or rules, which must be followed to form meaningful program statements.

3. Assembly language programs are converted into machine language by a special program called a(n) *assembler*.

4. Fourth-generation languages commonly are described as *nonprocedural*, which means programmers simply communicate what should be done instead of specifying the steps required.

5. A(n) *Application generator* is a *program builder* that produces programs in other languages.

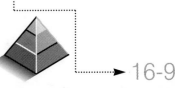

Examining the Issues

1. When computers were first introduced in schools, computer programming was routinely taught to students at all levels. As time passed, however, the emphasis in computer instruction turned toward application software. People felt programs had already been written for just about every imaginable task, and it was more important to teach students how to use the tools available. Today, however, that trend is changing. More educators are teaching programming languages such as COBOL, Visual Basic, C++, and Java. They believe that programming should still be an integral part of computer education. How might knowledge of programming benefit computer users? Should programming in some form be a part of computer education? Why or why not? To whom should programming be taught?

2. Because each programming language has its own strengths and weaknesses, different languages are used for different applications. Some authorities believe, however, it would be best to develop a single programming language that could be used for all applications. What would be the advantage of writing all applications using the same programming language? What would be the disadvantages? Will a *generic* programming language ever be developed? Why or why not?

Investigating the World

1. Some applications come with programming languages (sometimes called macro languages) that can be used to write programs within the application. For example, Microsoft Excel, a spreadsheet program, and Microsoft Word, a word processing program, both include Visual Basic for Applications (VBA). Visit a software vendor and find an application that contains a programming language. What is the name of the application? What is the name of the programming language? For what purpose is the language used? If possible, ask to see a demonstration of the programming language. Does it appear difficult to use? Why or why not? Would the inclusion of a programming language in an application be a factor in your decision whether or not to purchase the software? Why?

2. Careers in programming are hotter than ever: estimates anticipate that from the year 1992 to the year 2005 there will be a 30 percent increase in the number of programmer positions available. What knowledge and skills are required to land one of these jobs? Using classified ads from newspapers, computer magazines, trade journals, or other resources, try to determine what employers are looking for in prospective programmers. What programming languages are most in demand? What other skills and course work are required? What kind of experience is helpful? What are the programmer's responsibilities? What salary can be expected? What are the opportunities for advancement?

Keeping Your Computer Virus Free

17

Summarizing the Lab

Instructions: Use the *Keeping Your Computer Virus Free* interactive lab to complete the following outline.

I. What is a computer virus?

A computer virus is a _program_ designed to spread copies of itself to computer systems without detection. Once spread, it causes the infected computer systems to perform unwanted actions.

A survey of American companies with more than 200 personal computers showed that over 60 percent had suffered at least one viral attack. Because two of the major sources of viruses — illegally copied software and free software — are used more commonly by small companies and private PC users, the total percentage of PCs affected by viruses may be much higher.

> **Exploring Your Computer**
>
> Have you ever experienced problems with a virus on your computer? If so, were you able to successfully remove the virus? Is there a virus protection program, such as IBM AntiVirus, McAfee VirusScan, Cheyenne InocuLan, or Norton AntiVirus, running on your computer?

II. The process of virus infection

A computer virus is created by a programmer, then inserted into a piece of software.

A. Viruses invade a computer system by hiding within _data_ .

The three main types of viruses are: _Boot Sector Viruses_ ,
File Viruses , and _Trogen Horse Viruses_ .

1. A _Boot Sector Virus_ replaces the startup code on a disk with
   a modified version, which is loaded into memory when the computer is booted (started).

   From memory, the virus can infect any disk used by the computer.

2. A _File Virus_ attaches itself to a legitimate program
   file, where it intercepts the program's execution and takes
   control of the computer system.

   Viruses usually infect executable files, rather than data files, on a
   computer system.

3. A _Trogen Horse Virus_ is disguised to look like a legitimate
   program and is launched by an unsuspecting user, believing it is
   legitimate software.

   Frequently found on bulletin boards, these programs may appear
   to be utilities or games.

B. Once a virus has infected a computer, it uses the computer's
   resources to secretly _spread_ of itself, sometimes
   attaching copies to new data files.

   Viruses also copy themselves onto _any disk_ that is
   inserted into the computer's drive. Any computers that run the
   infected disk will also become infected. Viruses can multiply
   exponentially as users share infected files.

   School computer labs can be a particularly fertile breeding ground
   for viruses. One student with an infected application program disk
   can spread a virus to several laboratory computers, which in turn
   contaminate other students' application software.

C. Viruses are designed to become active at a specific point.

   The three main categories of viruses, based on the actions that
   trigger them, are illustrated in Figure 17.

1. A _Time Bomb_ is a virus that stops duplicating and
   becomes active when a certain date registers on the computer
   system's clock.

   Time bombs are sometimes a legitimate part of leased software.
   When the software is run, the program checks the date. If the
   date is past the terminal date of the lease, the software does not
   work.

   Halloween, April Fool's Day, and Friday the 13th are favorite
   days for viral attacks. Some companies routinely back up all
   software before these dates.

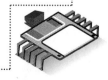

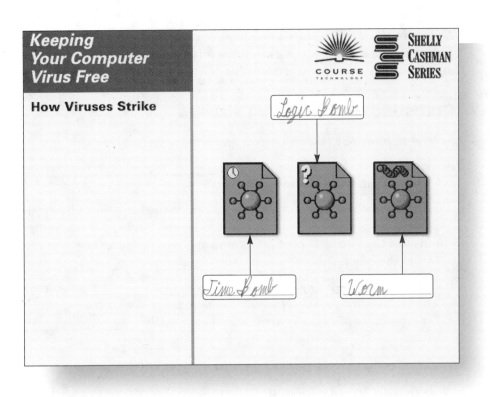

Figure 17

2. A *Logic Bomb* is triggered when a particular event occurs.

   Logic bombs are activated by the appearance or disappearance of certain data. For example, a disgruntled employee could insert a logic bomb that would go off if the employee's name is removed from the payroll file.

3. A *Worm* is a virus-like program that creates copies of itself continuously until the computer system is overloaded and stops working.

   Unlike a virus, worms do not need a host program. Worm programs enter a system through a computer network. In 1988, a worm created by a Cornell graduate student entered the Internet, affecting about 6,000 computers. A spokesperson claimed the worm cost NASA over 140 person-years of labor to eradicate.

III. Effects on the computer

A benign virus may announce itself with *unexpected messages* on the computer screen.

A more malicious virus may cause the computer to behave erratically or *freeze*.

Many viruses will corrupt or destroy valuable *data*.

A virus program can be just a few lines of code inserted in a legitimate program. When the program is run, the virus code can display an irritating comment, interrupt processing, or delete data from the hard disk.

IV. Detecting and removing viruses

Several steps can be taken to detect and remove viruses.

A. First, restart the computer using a ___rescue disk___, which is a startup disk that is known to be clean.

A virus removal program sometimes can be used to delete virus code from a program. If the infection is too severe, however, a rescue disk insures the virus has been eradicated and programs can be reinstalled from the original disks.

B. Next, an ___Anti-Virus___ or ___Vaccine___ program is run to look for program fragments that change boot sectors or the computer's operating system, which are usually ___read-only___ files.

Exploring Windows 95

New anti-virus programs are available that take advantage of the features Windows 95 offers. Some of the these anti-virus programs for Windows 95 are:

- Data Fellows's F-PROT Professional
- McAfee's VirusScan
- Symantec's Norton AntiVirus

Some anti-virus programs are designed to be run periodically, while others continually monitor system activity. Examples of anti-virus programs include Norton AntiVirus and Microsoft Anti-Virus. But, buyer beware — soon after a popular, inexpensive anti-virus program called Flu Shot IV came on the market, it was infected with a virus and offered for free on computer bulletin boards.

Anti-virus programs scan memory and files for ___virus signatures___, which are patterns of code from known viruses.

To avoid reinfection, every floppy disk used on a computer system should be checked with an anti-virus program. The search for virus signatures is fast; however, it is important to remember that only viruses with known signatures can be detected.

Anti-virus programs also can protect files against future infection by ___inoculating___, which involves recording file size and creation data so changes can be detected.

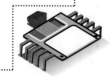

Using the recorded information, the vaccine program can tell if a virus program has tampered with the program file. Some anti-virus programs use a checksum — a value calculated by adding all the bytes in a file—which is reviewed each time the file is accessed to make sure the file has not been changed.

C. Several steps can be taken to prevent virus infection:

1. Install _Virus protection software_ to automatically check new files for viruses.

2. Use an _anti-virus program_ to scan disks for viruses before accessing them.

3. Check _new programs_ for viruses before running them.

4. Be especially careful with software posted to _computer bulletin boards, downloaded software or e-mail_ where many viruses first appear.

Exploring Online

Many Web sites offer information on anti-virus software and advice for protecting your computer against viruses. Some of these are:

- Data Fellows's Computer Virus Information page
- Stiller Research
- Symantec Anti-Virus Reference Center

To obtain more detals on viruses and anti-virus programs, visit the Exploring Computers Web page (www.scsite.com/expl.htm) and click Viruses.

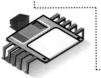

Evaluating the Results

True/False

Instructions: Circle **T** if the statement is true or **F** if the statement is false.

T F 1. Once a virus has infected a computer, it uses the computer's resources to secretly spread copies of itself.

T **F** 2. Viruses cannot copy themselves onto floppy disks inserted into the computer's disk drive.

T **F** 3. Worm programs wait for a specific event, and so are much more complicated than time bombs or logic bombs.

T **F** 4. Virus signature files rarely need to be updated.

T F 5. Inoculating a file involves recording a file's size and creation date so an anti-virus program can detect if the file is changed by a virus.

Matching

Instructions: Write the letter of a description from the column on the right in front of each term in the column on the left.

_b_ 1. Boot-sector virus

_7 ___ 2. Program virus

_d_ 3. Trojan horse virus

_e_ 4. Time bomb

_g_ 5. Logic bomb

a. intercepts execution when a legitimate program is run and takes control of the system *file virus*

b. replaces startup code on a disk with a modified version

c. repeatedly copies itself in memory or on a disk drive until no space remains *worm*

d. is disguised to look like a legitimate program, frequently found on bulletin boards

e. becomes active when a certain date registers on the computer system's clock

f. looks for program fragments that change the computer's operating system *anti-virus program*

g. triggered when a particular event occurs, such as an employee being terminated

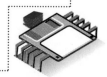

Multiple Choice

Instructions: Circle the correct response.

1. What does a virus do after invading a computer system?
   a. it takes control of the computer system
   b. it hides, waiting for a specific event to occur
   c. it damages hardware and peripheral devices
   d. it sets up permanent residence in memory

2. What type of virus is loaded into memory when the computer is started?
   a. boot-sector virus
   b. file virus
   c. program virus
   d. Trojan horse virus

3. Michelangelo's virus, which becomes active on March 6 (Michelangelo's birthday), is an example of what type of virus?
   a. logic bomb
   b. worm
   c. time bomb
   d. vaccine

4. What effect might a virus have on a computer?
   a. unexpected messages appear on the computer screen
   b. the computer behaves erratically or freezes
   c. valuable data is corrupted or destroyed
   d. all of the above

5. Which of the following is *not* a step that should be followed to prevent infection by a computer virus?
   a. install virus protection software
   b. use an anti-virus program
   c. check new programs for viruses after running them
   d. be especially careful with software posted to computer bulletin boards

Fill in the Blanks

Instructions: Place the correct word(s) in the blank in each sentence.

1. A(n) _computer virus_ is a program designed to spread copies of itself without detection to computer systems.

2. A(n) _Worm_ is a virus-like program that continuously copies itself until the computer system is overloaded and stops working.

3. If a virus is found, the computer should be restarted using a(n) _rescue disk_ to ensure that the computer is running without any viruses in memory.

4. A(n) _anti-virus program or vaccine_ looks for program fragments that change boot sectors of the computer's operating system, which are normally read-only files.

5. Anti-virus programs scan memory and files for patterns of code from known viruses, called _virus signatures_.

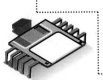

Examining the **Issues**

1. Computer viruses first appeared in the mid-1980s. Since then, viruses have ruined hospital records, wiped out bank registers, obliterated programs in thousands of personal computers, and cost businesses and government enormous amounts of money and numbers of work hours. Although a few viruses are created for personal gain or revenge against an organization, most viruses are launched without a specific target. Why do you think people create computer viruses? What, if anything, can be done to stop this malicious mischief?

2. In a famous case, Robert Morris was found guilty of infecting a computer network with a virus that damaged data and files for more than 6,000 users. Morris's sentence was 400 hours of community service, a three year probation, and a $10,000 fine. Some people feel this sentence was too lenient, given the extent of the harm the virus caused. Others believe Morris actually did the network a favor by demonstrating the limitations of its security system. Was the punishment appropriate? Why or why not? Would this punishment serve as a deterrent to other potential computer criminals?

Investigating the **World**

1. Of the thousands of known viruses, some have become particularly well known, either because of their effects on computer systems or as a result of their impact on computer users. Famous computer viruses include the ARPAnet data virus, the Scores virus, the Bell Labs virus, the brain virus, the Israeli virus, the Lehigh virus, the MacMag virus, the Stoned virus, the Friday the 13th virus, and the Michelangelo virus. Using a library or other research facility, prepare a brief report on any three viruses. What type of virus was each? How was it triggered? What was its effect? What impact did it have on computer users? Was the creator of the virus ever discovered? If so, how?

2. As with other software, when purchasing anti-virus programs it is important to buy software that suits your needs. Visit a computer vendor and find at least two anti-virus programs. What is the name of each? How much does each cost? With which type of computer (or operating system) does each work? How easy are they to use? How does each detect a virus? How many viruses can they detect? When was each last updated? Will there be future updates? If so, how much will the updates cost? After answering these questions, which program would you be more likely to buy? Why?

Understanding Multimedia

Summarizing the Lab

Instructions: Use the *Understanding Multimedia* interactive lab to complete the following outline.

I. What is multimedia?

Multimedia refers to any computer program that combines media elements such as text, graphics, animations, audio, and video. The basic elements of multimedia are shown in Figure 18.

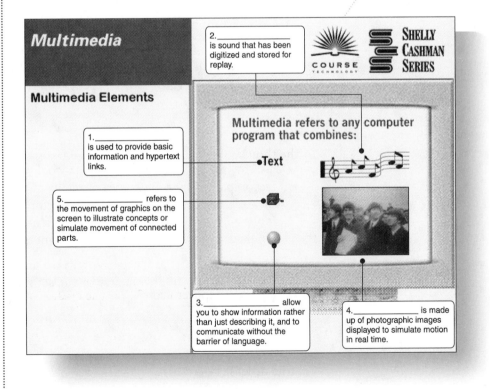

Figure 18

II. Interactivity

The most distinguishing features of multimedia are its _media elements_ and its _interactivity_. A multimedia application that accepts input from the user is called interactive multimedia. Interacting with multimedia applications usually requires a mouse or other pointing device, which is used to choose what material is presented and in what order.

Hyperlinks can be clicked to access information within a multimedia application in a nonlinear fashion. Hyperlinks can be _hypertext links_, which are text-based, or _hypermedia_, which are based on graphics or other media. Hypertext links are sometimes known as hotwords.

III. Multimedia elements

In multimedia applications, there usually some on-screen text displays along with hyperlinks that when clicked might:

- Playback an audio recording
- Display a graphic
- Playback a video demonstration
- Begin an animated simulation

A. Audio components

Multimedia PCs contain _sound cards_ that allow the audio used in a multimedia application to be recorded or played back. A sound card is a _circuit board_ with processors that provide both audio input and output.

Using _sound editing software_ with a sound card allows audio signals to be combined and recording and playback levels to be modified.

Sound is a powerful informational tool, whether used alone or accompanied by other types of media. The sounds of a beating heart, a native French speaker, or a symphony can be conveyed well only with audio capability. An actor's narration added to the text of a Shakespearean play can enhance understanding of the work.

Audio is sound that has been digitized and stored for replay. Two factors determine the quality of the sound heard when an audio file is played: _sampling rate_ and _resolution_ (in bits). In general, the higher the sound quality, the larger the audio file.

Exploring Windows 95

Windows 95 includes a Media Player to allow you to play audio, video, or animation files — even your favorite music CDs! The Media Player also allows you to control the settings for multimedia hardware devices such as speakers. To start the Media Player, click the Start button, point to Programs on the Start menu, and point to Accessories on the submenu. Point to Multimedia on the Accessories submenu and click Media Player. Choose the appropriate device (CD Audio, Video for Windows, and so on) and enjoy the show!

B. Graphics

Pictures allow information to be shown, rather than just described. Pictures also communicate without the barrier of language. People are more visually oriented than ever before — witness the popularity of television, movies, and highly visual magazines.

A graphic is a *digitized* image that can be displayed by a computer. Graphics can be purchased in clip art collections or created with a drawing software package. Photographs can be digitized with a scanner, captured with a digital camera, or purchased on CD-ROMs.

The graphics used in multimedia range from simple two-dimensional (2-D) drawings to intricate, photorealistic, three-dimensional (3-D) images.

1. The two dimensions of 2-D graphics are *width* and *height*. In multimedia applications, 2-D graphics often serve as objects that can be selected as hyperlinks.

2. 3-D graphics have the added dimension of *depth*. 3-D graphics are created using specialized software that shows greater levels of detail and makes images more realistic.

C. Video

Video is made up of photographic images displayed at rates of up to *30 frames* per second to simulate motion in real time. Video is widely used in multimedia applications designed for training.

Multimedia PCs have video capture cards and display adapters, which can be used to record and play back video clips.

Video must be converted from *analog* to *digital* to be used by a computer. Digital video files are very large. These files must be reduced in size to be accessed and managed by a computer. The process of reducing the size of a file and later expanding it for viewing is called *compression & decompression*.

Video compression takes advantage of the fact that only a small portion of the image changes from frame to frame. A compression program might store the first reference frame and then store only the changes from one frame to the next. The Moving Pictures Expert Group (MPEG) has developed compression methods that can reduce the size of video files up to 95 percent, while retaining near-television quality.

D. Animations

Animations refers to the movement of graphics on the screen. Animations can illustrate concepts more vividly than text or still graphics. An animation showing a piston valve opening and closing as it moves up and down provides a better depiction of how an internal combustion engine works than still pictures and a written description.

Three types of animations are:

1. *2D* are similar to 2-D graphics, except that they have movement.

2. *3D* provide the added dimension of perspective. 3-D animations can simulate the movement of connected parts. Even simple 3-D animations are created from detailed, computer-generated models and take a long time to create.

3. *Virtual Reality* uses computer-generated 3-D animation to simulate whole, interactive worlds. Interactive 3-D animations are created using *VRML*, which stands for *Virtual Reality Modeling Language*.

IV. Multimedia and the CD-ROM

CD-ROM technology has played an important role in the development of multimedia. Multimedia files often are too large to be stored practically on floppy disks. A CD-ROM, however can store about the same amount of data as *460* floppy disks.

CD-ROM drives with slower transfer rates often fail to fully integrate audio and video. Quad-speed or higher CD-ROM drives are needed to ensure smooth playback of multimedia files.

CD-ROMs have made the development and delivery of powerful multimedia applications possible and practical.

V. Multimedia personal computers

A *Multimedia Personal Computers (MPC)* has specific hardware and software components used to input, process, and output the media used in multimedia applications. MPCs often are referred to by their *MPC level*, a set of standards developed by several companies in the computer industry. The most recent level is *MPC Level 3*.

Components for which MPC Level 3 standards are:

- <u>*RAM*</u>
- <u>*CPU*</u>
- <u>*Hard Drive*</u>
- <u>*CD-ROM Drive*</u>
- <u>*Input & Output*</u> *Devices*
- <u>*Audio Components*</u>
- <u>*Video Components*</u>

Exploring Your Computer

Does your computer have any components of a multimedia PC? For instance, does it have a CD-ROM drive? Does it have a sound card and speakers? Are the speakers built into the computer or are they attached by a cable? Could your computer be considered an MPC Level 2 or 3 multimedia computer?

VI. Uses of multimedia

Multimedia is used in business and education for training, marketing, reference, entertainment, and more.

A. One application of multimedia is <u>*Computer-Based Training (CBT)*</u>, which is used to teach specific skills on the spot, instead of having employees attend outside workshops.

Interactive training software, called courseware can be distributed by CD-ROM or shared over a network.

B. Many businesses use multimedia to <u>*advertise*</u> and sell products and to create exciting <u>*marketing presentations*</u>. Multimedia software demos can be mailed as advertisements. The Internet is another way companies are delivering multimedia marketing and advertising materials.

Exploring Online

Some of the most exciting applications of multimedia today are happening on the World Wide Web. The Virtual Neighbourhood, for example, is a virtual Web city with an apartment complex, a park, a theater, and more. The site, which was created in VRML, is designed to demonstrate the value of virtual reality on the Web for businesses like real estate, retail, entertainment, and tourism. Other sites, such as The Multimedia Authoring Web, provide background information on authoring tools and links to multimedia research centers at colleges and universities worldwide. For more details on multimedia, visit the Exploring Computers Web page (www.scsite.com/expl.htm) and click Multimedia.

C. Many public places have computerized reference centers, called _information kiosks_, which are used to find specific information or browse through choices. Information kiosks often use _touch screen_ monitors that allow users to make selections by touching the appropriate area on the screen.

D. Many books, magazines, and reference texts are available in an interactive multimedia format. The pages of an electronic book are _turned_ by clicking icons. Multimedia magazines use many types of media to convey information. _Microsofts Encarta_ is a complete CD-ROM encyclopedia that uses graphics, animation, audio, and video to accompany the text. Digital texts usually contain hyperlinks to additional information.

E. Interactive multimedia computer games use _graphics_, _sound_, and _video_ to create a realistic, entertaining game. Often, the game simulates a real or fictitious world, in which the player takes the role of a character and has control of what happens. Some new multimedia products provide edutainment, an experience meant to be both educational and entertaining.

Evaluating the **Results**

True/False

Instructions: Circle **T** if the statement is true or **F** if the statement is false.

T **F** 1. Multimedia hyperlinks can be hypertext links, which are text-based, or hypermedia links, which are based on graphics or other media.

T **F** 2. Video must be converted from digital to analog to be used by a computer.

T **F** 3. Digital video files are very small and must be expanded in size so the computer can access and manage the files.

T **F** 4. Simple 3-D animations, like a bouncing ball, are produced with basic paint programs and take very little time to create.

T **F** 5. A multimedia personal computer (MPC) has specific hardware and software components used to input, process, and output the media used in multimedia applications.

Matching

Instructions: Write the letter of a description from the column on the right in front of each term in the column on the left.

_g_ 1. Computer-based training (CBT)

_b_ 2. Marketing and advertising

_a_ 3. Information kiosks

_f_ 4. Encyclopedia and references

_d_ 5. Multimedia games

a. located in many public places to help people find specific facts or browse through choices

b. many companies are using the Internet to deliver these multimedia materials

c. used to record daily occurrences, events, meetings, and reminders

d. often simulate a real or fictitious world in which users play the role of a character

e. compares a company's sales to its expenses and calculates net profit or loss

f. multimedia versions usually contain hyperlinks to more information, such as definitions or video

g. used to teach specific skills on the spot, instead of having employees attend outside workshops

►18-7

Multiple Choice

Instructions: Circle the correct response.

1. What are the most distinguishing features of multimedia?
   a. its reliance on a single medium and its inactivity
   b. its simplicity and its need for a variety of input devices
   c. its combination of media elements and its interactivity
   d. its banality and its insignificant system requirements

2. What are the two dimensions of 2-D graphics?
   a. width and height
   b. height and depth
   c. depth and weight
   d. weight and width

3. What do sampling rate and resolution (in bits) determine?
   a. the rate at which text files are transferred from memory
   b. the quality of the sound heard when an audio file is played
   c. the clarity of an animation or video file when it is decompressed
   d. the time it takes to empty a bag of potato chips at a fraternity party

4. Why has CD-ROM technology played an important role in the development of multimedia?
   a. the durability of CD-ROMs has made it possible to transport multimedia applications anywhere
   b. the large storage capacity of CD-ROMs has made multimedia applications possible and practical
   c. the adaptability of CD-ROMs has allowed users to make changes to multimedia applications
   d. the availability of CD-ROMs has made interactive multimedia applications viable in any setting

5. For what components does the MPC Level 3 set minimum requirements?
   a. RAM and CPU
   b. hard drive and CD-ROM drive
   c. input and output devices
   d. all of the above

Fill in the Blanks

Instructions: Place the correct word(s) in the blank in each sentence.

1. _Multimedia_ refers to any computer program that combines media elements such as text, graphics, animations, audio, and video.

2. Multimedia PCs contain _sound cards_, which are circuit boards housing processors that provide both audio input and output.

3. _Virtual Reality_ uses computer-generated 3-D animations to simulate whole, interactive worlds.

4. Multimedia personal computers often are referred to by their _M.P.C Levels_ which is a set of hardware and software standards developed by several companies in the computer industry.

5. Information kiosks often use _touch screen_ monitors that let selections be made by contacting the appropriate area on the screen.

Examining **the** **Issues**

1. Designing a multimedia application includes developing a project script that provides a written record of how various media elements will be used. For each frame in a multimedia application, the script describes the text, graphics, animation, audio, and interactivity (what users will do and the application response). Some guidelines for effective multimedia applications are:

   - Know the audience (tailor the application to meet users' needs).

   - Give users control (allow users to choose their own course).

   - Immerse the user (recreate tasks users must perform).

   - Require interaction (ask questions and provide feedback).

   - Review concepts (incorporate self-building exercises).

   - Engage the user (make the application attractive and appealing to the eye and ear).

   Write a short script for a multimedia application on a subject of your choice. Assume the application will use at least ten frames. Include descriptions of the multimedia elements in each frame.

2. Multimedia applications, particularly in the form of computer-based training (CBT), are assuming an increasingly important role in education. Advocates claim multimedia applications make learning more interesting, allow students to perform in a risk-free environment, provide instant feedback, and appeal to different learning styles. CBT offers reduced learning time, self-paced study, one-on-one interaction, decreased learning costs, and unique instructional experiences. Some supporters propose radically different classrooms with multimedia applications providing the bulk of the learning experience. Instead of being a _sage on the stage,_ the teacher would _guide on the side_, circulating among students and offering individual help. What advantages of CBT are most important? Why? What are the disadvantages of CBT? For what subjects is CBT most appropriate? Why? Will the radical vision of a classroom dedicated to CBT ever be realized? Why or why not?

Investigating the World

1. The development of interactive multimedia applications involves the use of multimedia authoring software. These programs combine text, graphics, animation, audio, and video and incorporate interactivity into a finished multimedia application. Three popular multimedia authoring programs are ToolBook (from Asymetrix Corporation), Authorware Professional (from Macromedia Inc.), and Director (from Macromedia Inc.). Each program uses a different metaphor (comparison) to make authoring easier: ToolBook uses a book metaphor, Authorware uses a flowchart metaphor, and Director uses a theater metaphor. Visit a software vendor and ask for a demonstration of a multimedia authoring program. What are the system requirements? How compatible is the program with other applications? Is the program easy to use? Why or why not? What functions does it perform? What technical support is offered? How good is the application developed?

2. A broad category of multimedia reference books is how-to guides. These interactive applications help people deal with tasks they face in their daily lives. The Reader's Digest *Complete Do-It-Yourself Guide* offers hundreds of home repair how-to tips. Animated *tours* also are provided that show ways to a beautiful home. The *Williams-Sonoma Guide to Good Cooking* is a multimedia cookbook. In addition to more than 1,000 recipes, the CD-ROM includes a search function that locates dishes with specific characteristics, a menu planner, and video tips. Microsoft's *Automap Streets Plus* is a multimedia travel guide. Information is offered on hotels, restaurants, museums, and tourist centers. Road maps show addresses throughout the United States. Visit a software vendor or resource center and try a multimedia how-to guide. What information does it provide? How easy is it to use? What advantages does it have over a printed guide? What are the disadvantages? How could the guide be improved?

Index